KU-195-570

Pictures and Words

New Comic Art and Narrative Illustration

by Roanne Bell and Mark Sinclair

Yale University Press

Jason from Mjau Beibi (Meow Baby), 2002

WITHDRAWN

LIVERPOOL JMU LIBRARY

3 1111 01362 3630

Contents 👉

Foreword p6

Silent
Introduction p10
Mr Clement p11
Jordan Crane p14
Martin tom Dieck p16
Tom Gauld p21
Jason p22
James Jarvis p26
Andrzej Klimowski p28
Ethan Persoff p31
David Shrigley p35
Jim Woodring p36

Single Panel
Introduction p40
Anna Bhushan p41
Barry Blitt p44
Paul Davis p46
Marcel Dzama p50
Scott Garrett p54
Tom Gauld p55
Simone Lia p57
Roderick Mills p61
David Shrigley p64
Andrew Wightman p65
Jim Woodring p66

Text and Image
Introduction p68
Fredrik von Blixen p69
Jordan Crane p72
Martin tom Dieck p74
Jeff Fisher p76
Tom Gauld p78
Jochen Gerner p82
Sammy Harkham p88
Igort p92
Benoît Jacques p96
Jason p100
Simone Lia p102
Lorenzo Mattotti p105
David Rees p108
Barnaby Richards p110
Jenni Rope p114
Joe Sacco p117
Marjane Satrapi p121
David Shrigley p125
Singh & Dunning p128
Katja Tukiainen p130

Artists' Biographies p135

Acknowledgements and Credits p144

Foreword 👉

"Constructing a comic strip is like looking at yourself in water but then leaving your reflection behind. You often go back and visit, and although you recognize the characters you've created, you are not always sure what they are up to, just as you can be surprised by your own face. Of course, you can make suggestions, and occasionally edit their actions, but that is the responsibility of being a creator."
Barnaby Richards, comics artist

Last year, a 1937 first edition of The Dandy comic sold for £20,350 to an anonymous UK bidder, the highest price ever paid for a British comic at auction. Comic Book Postal Auctions, which arranged the sale, revealed that the comic's value was in part due to its being in mint condition but, more so, that after nearly 67 years it still had its free gift attached. Out of the ten known surviving copies of the first edition, from the stable of the legendary DC Thompson publishing house in Dundee, Scotland, this was the only one to have endured exactly as it was originally sold.

The free gift, incidentally, was a toy "metal whistler". Together with the attached first edition, it undoubtedly made for a unique and highly collectable piece of comics history. Yet while this is true, the import of the survival of both comic and toy seems to reinforce that old misplaced adage that devotees of comic-book culture, artists and illustrators alike still hear all too often: that comics are just for kids. It's an accusation that comic-book art and, more generally, narrative illustration have seemingly battled against throughout their history. Only relatively recently have they started to receive the recognition and status as an art form that they deserve.

For some time now, narrative illustration (illustration that tells a story in its own right rather than just supporting another medium) has steadfastly moved away from simply being a vehicle for slapstick or superheroes. Fundamentally, comic books are a medium, not a genre, and one that engages superbly with any number of themes from the political – Pulitzer Prize-winning Art Spiegelman and cartoonist / journalist Joe Sacco are key proponents of this kind of work – to the historical and biographical. A book like Chris Ware's Jimmy Corrigan: The Smartest Kid on Earth, for example, has become a twenty-first century Bildungsroman, jumping about through America's last one hundred years via the personal history of its protagonist.

Of course, groundbreaking work has reared its head many times during the history of the medium. The recent, and long-overdue, revival of popular and critical interest in George Herriman's long-running Krazy Kat strips from the first half of the twentieth century, for example, has focused the attention of both contemporary artists and readers on examples of work that once challenged the very medium itself while all around cartooning was relatively staid and formulaic.

In recent years, the discipline of illustration as a whole has enjoyed a huge renaissance. Today, it holds an important place across all creative media, crossing boundaries between artistic disciplines: from book and magazine editorial, design and fashion, to advertising and film. In the latter, illustrated characters have featured frequently within many contemporary high-profile feature films. Waking Life, Spun and, more recently, Kill Bill have all incorporated animated sequences into live-action frameworks, while wholly animated films like Spirited Away and Belleville Rendezvous have become critical and box-office successes.

Narrative illustration is in the public eye more than ever. Previously, its status has been that of an essentially underground medium, rarely seen outside of comic books and magazines. Now, however, narrative illustration exists within a much wider, mainstream consciousness, with "graphic novels" occupying book critics' recommended-reading lists and comic art becoming the subject of week-long festivals and gallery exhibitions dedicated to the medium. Jimmy Corrigan received the Guardian First Book Award in 2001 – the first comic book to win such a literary prize – while more recent titles such as the two-volume Persepolis by Iranian artist Marjane Satrapi and Palestine by the Maltese-born itinerant comic-book journalist Joe Sacco are regarded as being, in the tradition of Spiegelman's Maus, hugely significant and politically charged works.

Established publishing houses are also keen to embrace narrative illustration in the UK: Faber & Faber published The Secret and The Depository by acclaimed artist Andrzej Klimowski, while booksellers, too, are wiser to the increasing appeal of the medium to contemporary readers, often including titles within broader, pre-existing Fiction or History sections or creating new, dedicated Graphic Novel areas (although regrettably some bookshops, still apparently unaware of the range of works now being produced, resolutely commit their entire stock of narrative illustration to their Humour sections).

Comica, an annual exhibition of comics art first held in 2003 at London's Institute of Contemporary Arts, has established a programme bursting with presentations by both leading international artists and younger, less-established talent, capturing the zeitgeist for narrative illustration in the UK; while in Europe and the US, the traditional comics festival circuit continues to thrive in places as diverse as Angoulême and Seattle. The cultural influence of cartoons and comic strips on art has been investigated recently in Splat, Boom, Pow! at Boston's Institute of Contemporary Arts, while a retrospective of the work of the US painter Philip Guston at London's Royal Academy also brought to the fore the significance of cartoon art to the artist's aesthetic development.

Narrative illustration itself has become a regular feature of the gallery world, which has provided precious support in accepting this kind of illustrated work as a legitimate art form. Fine artists Marcel Dzama and David Shrigley are key examples of this growing cultural crossover: gallery exhibitions of their illustrations and paintings attract legions of fans who have been captivated by their bleak and tangential narratives. Shrigley also recently completed a music video for the UK band Blur in which his illustrations were animated to tell a rather tragic and disturbing tale of life, love and death.

As a subject for an anthology, narrative illustration reveals two distinct strands: the telling of a story through pictures and words (images and text), and through pictures alone ("silent" images with no supporting text or speech). In addition, artists can reduce the actual narrative space of a story to a single frame. Many graphic novelists also employ pictorial or wordless passages within a larger body of work of text and image-based strips, and vice versa.

Norwegian comic artist Jason and US artist Jim Woodring are famed for drawing strips where the narrative develops through gestures alone. Typical of their existential drawings are the weight and universality of characters' expressions: their emotional states are depicted through their actions rather than spoken language. French artist Jochen Gerner goes further in removing everything but symbols from his work, as in the story featured here. His pieces are like a flow of colourful signs on a blackboard – rather than a linear sequence – from which a pictorial narrative emerges.

This book aims to explore the various uses of images with and without text – in single-panel pieces, in small strips of sequential panels and in longer sequences from larger stories. For instance, what particular effect can a comic artist achieve by suddenly switching to solely pictorial storytelling after pages of pictures with text in which the voice of a narrator or protagonist is carefully built up? How does the use of such a technique affect the reader's sense of time and the pacing of a work? How can it alter perspective or emotion?

Narrative illustration is evolving with great determination at the moment. Now increasingly acknowledged as a serious art form in its own right, it is breaking new ground by showing itself as a valid form of expression for a vast range of subjects, from socio-political issues to the most complex of human emotions. This book is a collection of some of the most outstanding work being produced in the field of narrative illustration at the moment: pictorial storytelling with, or without, words.

Silent

Mr Clement p11
Jordan Crane p14
Martin tom Dieck p16
Tom Gauld p21
Jason p22
James Jarvis p26
Andrzej Klimowski p28
Ethan Persoff p31
David Shrigley p35
Jim Woodring p36

Silent pictorial narration is an age-old art form and tool of communication. Its roots lie as far back in time as 35000BC in the form of cave paintings. Later, hieroglyphics inscribed inside the great pyramids, around 1300BC, were used to immortalize Egyptian rulers while more recently, in 400BC, Greek and Roman rulers were similarly celebrated in marble carvings around the sides of ancient structures. The Romans were also responsible for the earliest strip to be committed to paper, in the Quedlinburg Itala gospel book of Samuel. Later, the 230-foot-long Bayeux Tapestry of the Middle Ages told the story of the Norman invasion of England in 1066. In 1511, one of the largest sequential stories in picture form, Michelangelo's Sistine Chapel ceiling, was created, at the same time that narrative strips, usually in the form of woodcuts, were becoming a popular medium in Europe for the expression of religious and political ideas during the Reformation. The latter were themselves a crude and inexpensive version of a technique first developed in the East during the ninth century.

Modern comic art can perhaps claim the etchings and engravings of British painter and printmaker William Hogarth (1697–1764) as their main ancestors. Depicting and commenting on Georgian society, Hogarth's work went on to influence British satirists George Cruikshank (1756–1820), Thomas Rowlandson (1756–1827) and James Gillray (1757–1815), though these last two also adopted the speech balloon in their work. At the beginning of the twentieth century, Belgian artist Frans Masereel (1889–1972) pioneered a genre of book called the "woodcut novel", or the "novel without words". Masereel's beautiful oeuvres were made up of a series of woodcuts, printed one to a page, and are arguably the precursor to the modern graphic novel.

Today there are several different ways in which an illustrator or comic artist might choose to exploit the use of silence in a narrative. Aside from the obvious advantage of a narrative not told in any particular language and therefore immediately understandable to an international audience – Tom Gauld's silent piece entitled Settle, for example, was published in Switzerland, then distributed across Europe – there is often something more atmospheric, more enigmatic, about a silent narrative. Panels with words in them convey a sense of time's passage; the events take as long as the copy takes to read.

Readers of silent narratives, however, are expected to use their own imagination to fill in the blanks and guide the narrative. In Andrzej Klimowski's graphic novel The Depository, for instance, itself a descendant of Masereel's novels without words, the reader is made to work hard to uncover the storyline. It is precisely this lack of copy, and with it the lack of any sense of linear time or space, which provides the spooky atmosphere that is so important to the story's success. To add text would be to bring the narrative back into a safer, more understandable world and the story would lose its magical quality. Says Tom Gauld of this last point: "I think that because we are so used to reading words, we find them reassuring to have in comics, and sometimes this is bad as some readers can just skim over the pictures to get to the next set of words. In a story told entirely with pictures, especially in one-image-per-page books like Klimowski's or Masereel's, the reader is being asked to look into the pictures more to find the story, and the narrative can be more abstract or poetic."

There is of course a difference between a silent passage in a comic that elsewhere features sound and a story that is entirely silent. In Jordan Crane's story Keeping Two, for example, the sounds of different electrical appliances are used to highlight the silence of a particular sequence, and thus to heighten the tension and emotion. Similarly, in Ethan Persoff's A Dog and his Elephant, the silence of the passage is evident in that the only sounds present are the electric whir of a fridge and the clicking open or shutting of doors. Interestingly, however, Persoff takes this idea a step further in the second of his comics showcased here, entitled Teddy, by including speech bubbles but deliberately leaving these blank. The emotional charge and sense of hopelessness present during this conversation are highlighted by this technique.

Mr Clement

The opening of Mr Clement's surrealist tale sets the tone for this largely wordless story. When words finally do appear, they are printed on the reverse of the page that the text refers to, making for an interesting effect: the empty speech bubbles imply a dialogue that is only confirmed when the page is turned.

In the very first scene, Astrolapin seemingly waits for a reply to his letter and experiences feelings of frustration and violence at the environment around him. At one point, he walks out of the story altogether, escaping through one of the frames, as if the fragmented nature of the tale enables him to climb out through a crack.

from The Gorgeous Habour, 2004

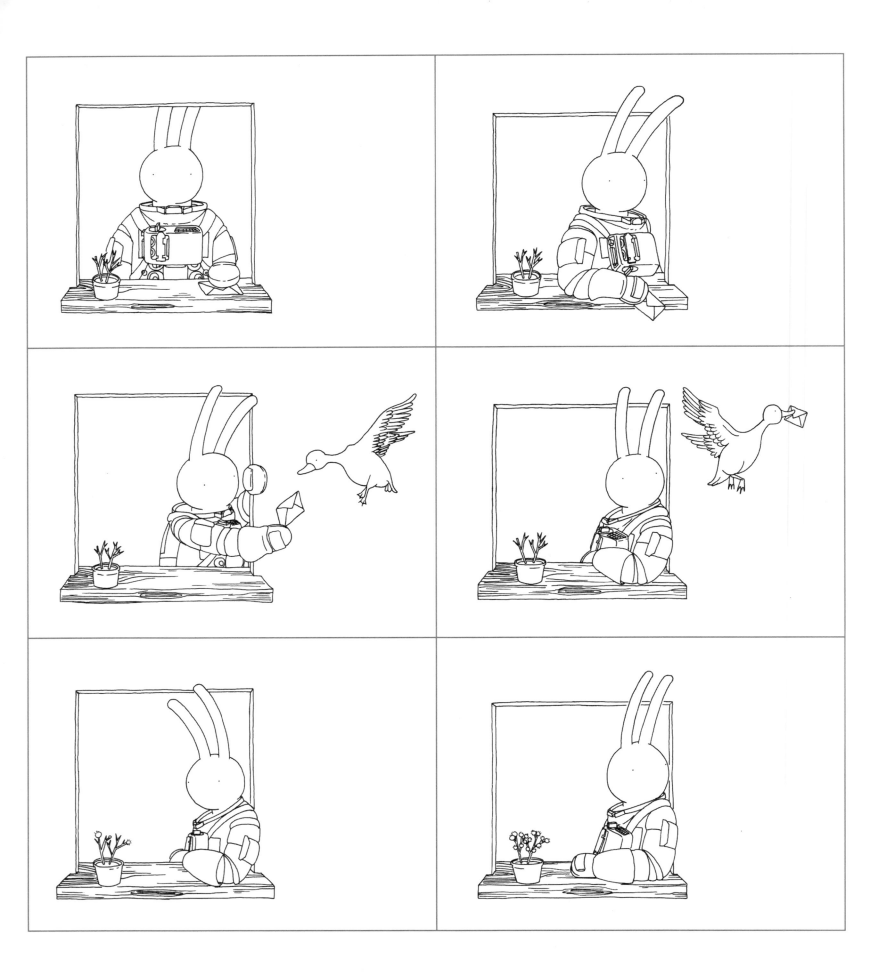

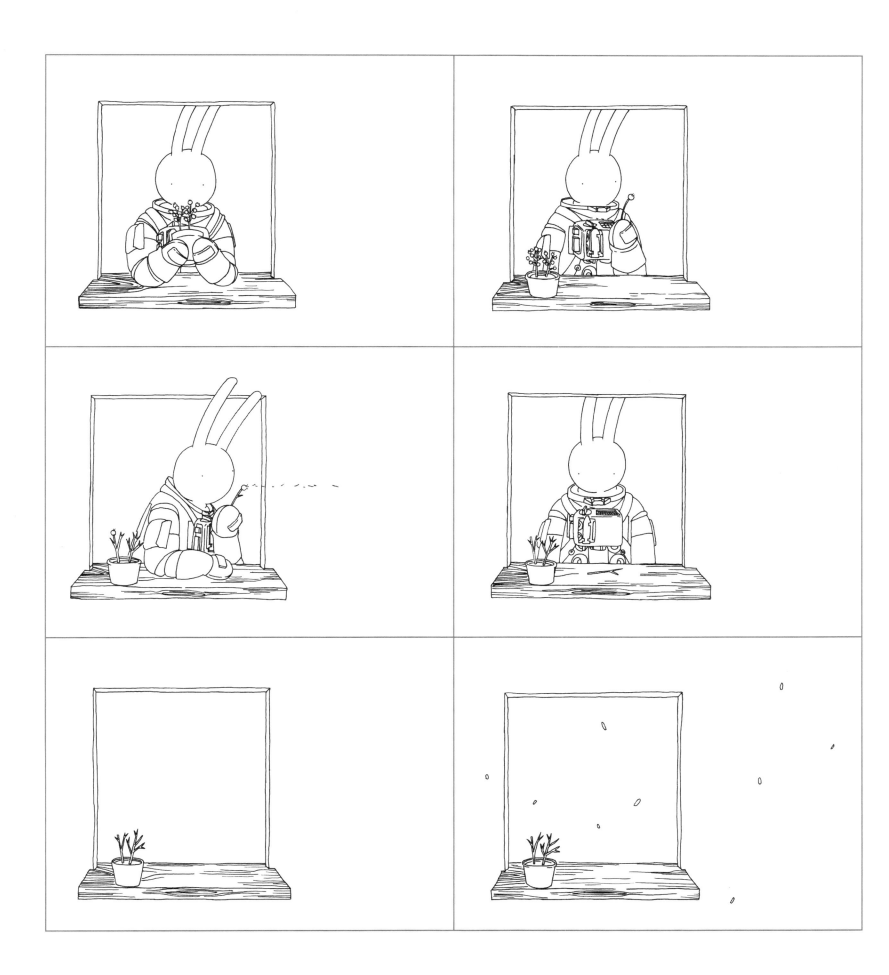

Crane's Keeping Two story begins with a young man called Will returning home from a road trip with his girlfriend Maggie. While he washes the dishes, he remembers the story that she has just read to him in the car about a couple whose child is stillborn while the husband is away on business. The news is devastating for the couple in the story: the man returns to work and the woman is left alone in the house. Life ticks over in his office while at home the woman occupies herself with chores and cups of coffee.

Crane shows how, despite the tragedy, life goes on – the silent narrative is dotted with black marks of background noise and everyday sounds, and the absence of text sharpens the keenness of the unexpressed emotion. The only human sound in the sequence comes in the final panel – a solitary "sob" is the only gesture of speech to break the silence.

Martin tom Dieck

La FM is a series of three short stories. Tom Dieck describes these pieces as "short expeditions into disparate themes" which he created when he found the work he'd been doing on a larger, unfinished story becoming "quite overbearing". The La FM title that encompasses the three stories apparently loosely references this larger, ongoing project but also, he explains, hints at the impressionistic nature of the stories themselves.

"For the first part I thought it could be a reference to the radio wavelength, and what you see are imaginations of what you might hear when quickly crossing between channels," says the artist. The second part was completed for a "frontiers"-themed issue of Satellite International, a Portuguese magazine. It apparently featured at least three stories about car crashes.

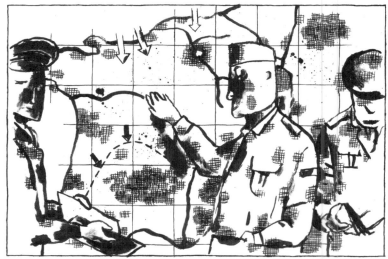

The silent third part of La FM was published in Beaux-Arts magazine in Paris and also in issue 75 of German comics magazine Strapazin, where, tom Dieck notes, "it was preceded by a story by Dominique Goblet that also ended with a girl walking on a pavement. Our styles are completely different, but they appear as two sides of the same thing. I prefer to leave La FM enigmatic."

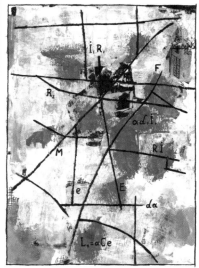

Shown here in its entirety, Settle is a small pictorial comic book, measuring just 3×4cm (1.13×1.57in). It was produced for the Swiss publishers Bulb as part of a series of individual sets of five concertina comics in boxes. Gauld's silent piece seems to be a subtle narrative on the process of urbanization.

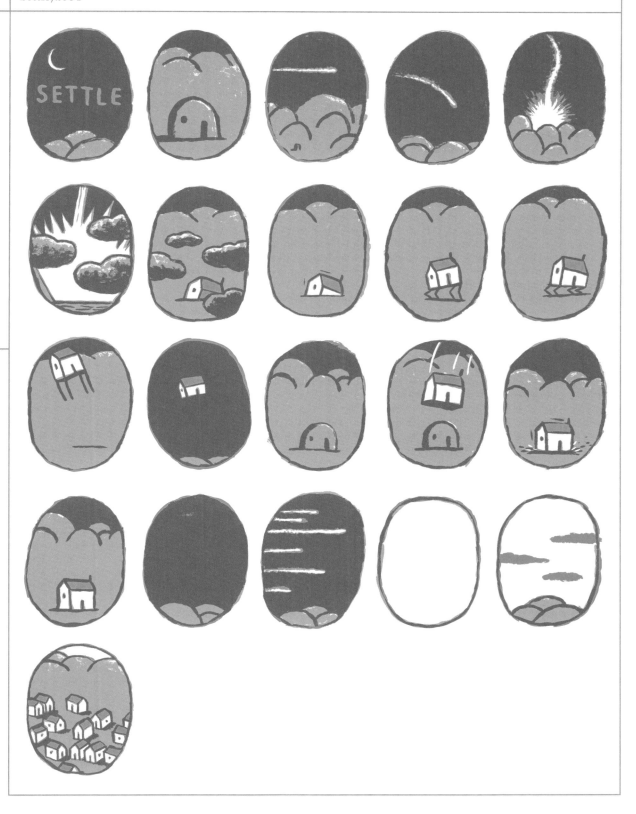

LIVERPOOL JOHN MOORES UNIVERSITY
LEARNING SERVICES

The simplicity of Jason's Mjau Beibi comics (published by Jippi Forlag) derives from his intention to work within the confines of a strip format and, as he says, "to tell a funny story within three or four panels. I have a great respect for those who can do it, like Charles Schulz or Berkeley Breathed." Jason has a keen eye for universal human activities (changing on the beach; the middle-of-the-night journey to the fridge; sheltering from rain) and his wordless panels convey an instantly recognizable action or expression. The use of "types" in his stories is further reinforced by his use of animal heads for his characters. "I guess I try to tell a story in images or a combination of words and images, and not strictly in words, which often is the case of modern newspaper strips," he says. "Also, it's in order to be able to reach out to the newspaper readers who normally don't buy comics."

MJAU BEÏBI *av jason*

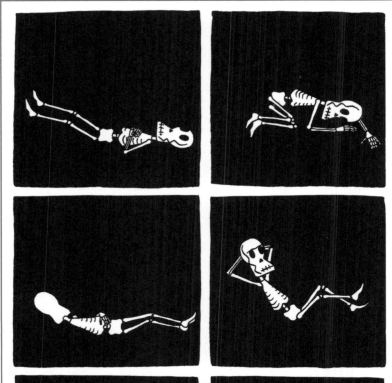

World of Pain is a self-contained universe created by Jarvis to house some of his potato-headed characters. In this silent comic, the behaviour of the characters is constantly controlled by means of the street signs and the presence of the long arm of the law. Jarvis's more recent illustrative work and, indeed, his numerous vinyl toys have evolved a range of other characters. He is therefore now planning to create more of what he terms a "multiverse", where the different characters from different worlds can coexist.

The framing devices in World of Pain emphasize the environment's claustrophobic nature – characters cannot go far out of view of the police. In this extract, in fact, the law is present in every panel (even if its representative has taken to skateboarding in a few of them).

from World of Pain, 2000

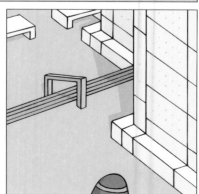

Andrzej Klimowski

Andrzej Klimowski's wordless novel The Depository: A Dream Book was originally published by Faber & Faber in 1994, and more recently in 2001 in a Polish edition by Slowo/Obrez Terytoria Gdansk entitled Magazyn Snów (Storehouse of Dreams). The novel came about after a planned literary festival for which Klimowski had created a logo of a flying man with an open book protruding from his shoulder blades in place of wings was cancelled. With his wife, artist Danusia Schejbal, Klimowski had also created drawings of the flying man, and later a flying woman, which were to be made into lifesize sculptures to promote the event.

Explains Klimowski: "The 'literary angels' never did land in the shops but they started to live a life of their own through a series of drawings and linocut prints that I continued to produce. I had so many of these images pinned to the studio wall and I realized that somewhere amongst them there was a latent story waiting to be pieced together."

"I made a few notes and decided to work methodically by disciplining myself in going to the reference library and clocking in a regular four hours of work every day. On the first day I immediately experienced writer's block. There I was with my sketchbook, a pot of ink, brushes and pencil, but I was unable to make a mark. After a while I just drew what was in front of me: the back of a man sitting at a desk, leaning over a book. He was like me; trying to write. This is how the story started. It continued in a stream of consciousness right to the very last page."

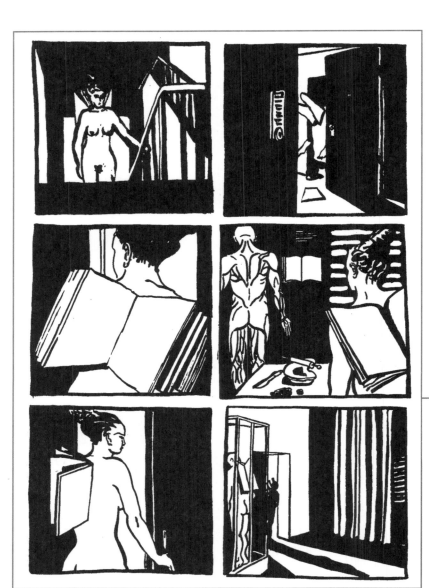

Taking place in a one-room apartment, A Dog and his Elephant is the story of Frank and his girlfriend Eleanor. It is told using a fixed-perspective camera view ("similar to a 1950s television comedy set," says Persoff), the single-angle approach adding to the sense of distance from the action that the reader feels when viewing this abusive relationship. Silence is conveyed very literally here: in some sequences the only noise present is the electric whir of the fridge and the clicking open or shutting of doors. Time passes slowly as Persoff emphasizes the claustrophobic nature of the relationship and the feeling of entrapment by changing the action minimally from panel to panel. The complete story can be read on Persoff's website, www.ep.tc.

from **A Dog and his Elephant**, 2003

An unconventional love story, Teddy is a silent tale involving a picnic, drink-driving and a car crash that catapults the strange relationship between Teddy, his girl and their adopted child, Clod, towards a tragic ending. Persoff portrays all the action wordlessly and cleverly underlines those points where the most heightened and emotionally intense speech would be taking place by incorporating blank speech bubbles. These empty indicators of speech add a sense of hopelessness and inevitability to the content of the imaginary dialogue between the characters.

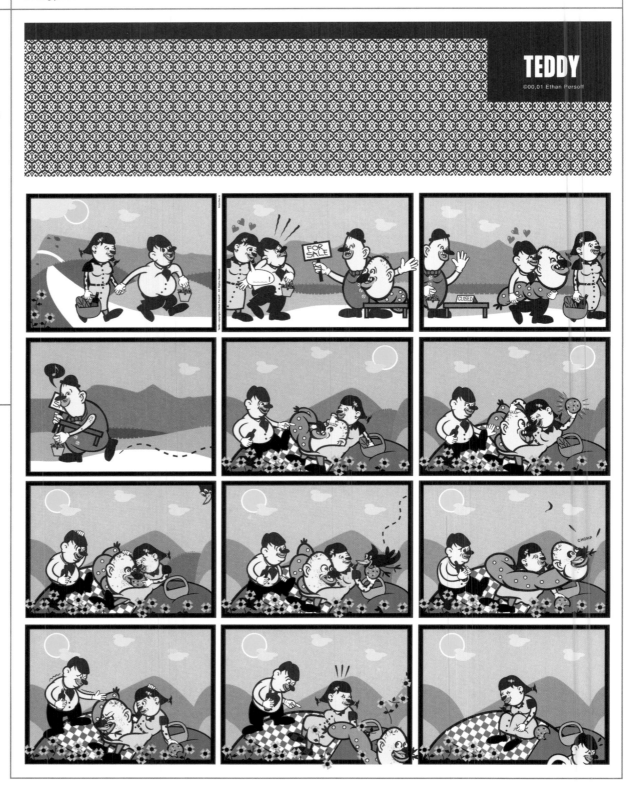

UK-based artist David Shrigley creates his surreal drawings with a simple toolkit of pen, pencil and paper. Anybody struggling with the contradictions of modern life and the nonsensical aspects of the human condition can take solace from his work. Shown here is a day in the life of an executioner as rendered silently in Shrigley's understated trademark style.

"All my work deals with the same sorts of things," says Woodring; "invisible forces, inexplicable relationships, unintentional catalytic effects, and the speculation about what lies behind the necessary obfuscation of consensus reality."

Woodring expressed these kinds of "potent but elusive ideas" in a traditional cartoon vocabulary in his acclaimed Frank comics. "To do this I tried to remove every trace of time or place so as to keep the storyline isolated from any specific culture," he says. "This included avoiding language, so that the actions and events would be as 'universal' as possible."

Pupshaw and Pushpaw are two of the characters from this strange world. One of their silent adventures formed the basis for the eponymous book, published by Presspop Gallery in Japan. Created for children and limited to just 12 pages, Woodring admits that "most of my usual techniques – longer stories, an atmosphere of menace, occasional shockingly gruesome events – were out."

from Pupshaw and Pushpaw, 2004

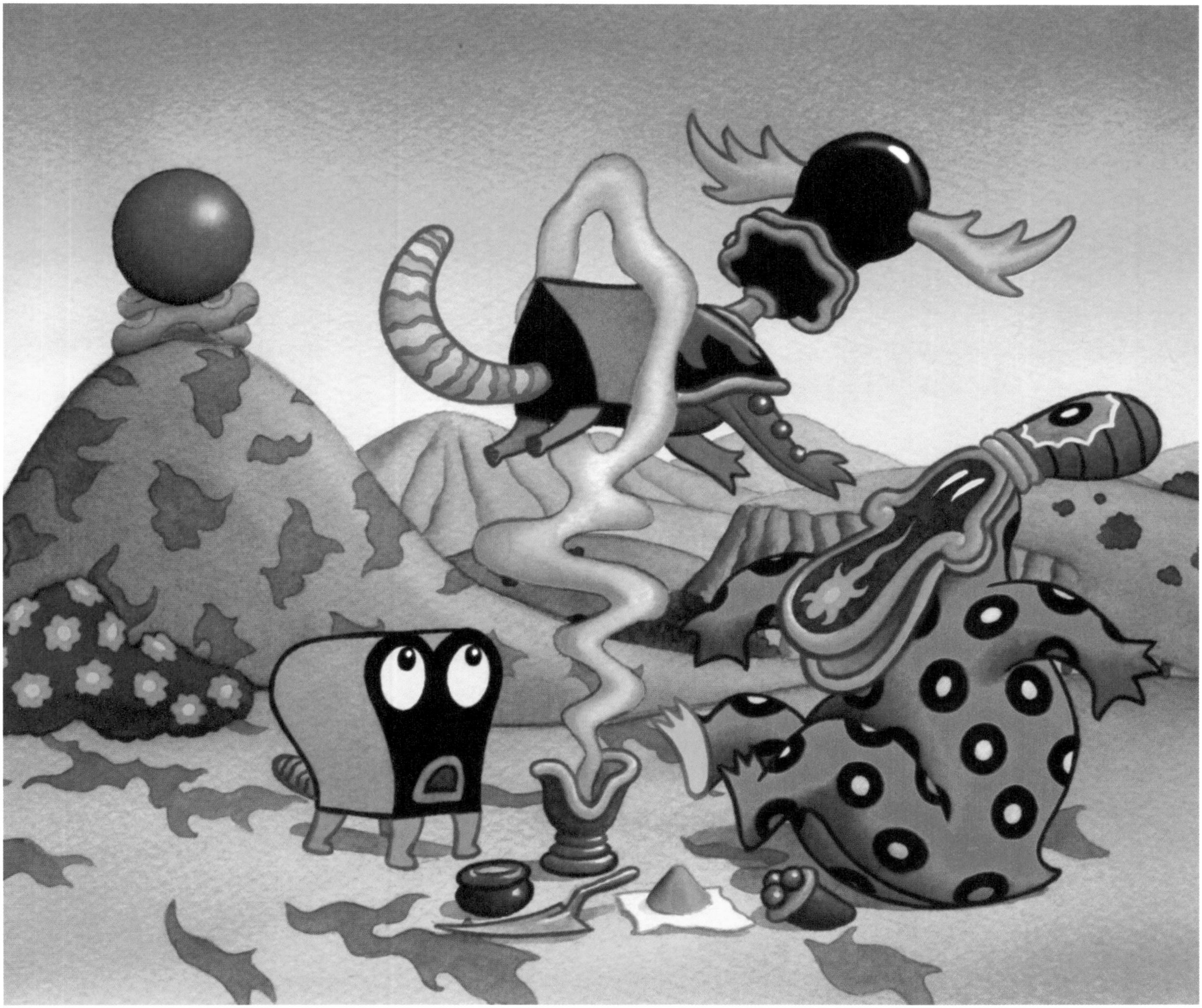

Single Panel 👉

Anna Bhushan **p41**
Barry Blitt **p44**
Paul Davis **p46**
Marcel Dzama **p50**
Scott Garrett **p54**
Tom Gauld **p55**
Simone Lia **p57**
Roderick Mills **p61**
David Shrigley **p64**
Andrew Wightman **p65**
Jim Woodring **p66**

The single-panel work has its roots in the earliest incarnations of the cartoon illustration, the precursor to the comic strip. The type of cartoons that first appeared in La Charivari in France, then Punch in the UK and, later, Harper's Illustrated Weekly in the US during the nineteenth century, for example, were vehicles for political satire and aimed to capture, as newspaper cartoons still do today, a contemporary issue or convey the nature of a particular figure – more often than not disparagingly – through a single page drawing and line of text (which was often direct speech).

By its very nature, the single panel denies any pictorial sense of "before" or "after" but instead captures a moment in time, using it to tell a larger story. Canadian artist Marcel Dzama sets up surrealistic situations in his illustrative work, while in many of UK artist David Shrigley's drawings, a succinct narrative exists within a single frame or panel, which remains a story all the same (albeit a bizarre one).

In one of Shrigley's most affecting drawings (reproduced on page 64), the word "joy" triumphantly adorns a portrait of a rather smug, beaming figure, but then a series of smaller words follow on beneath the image – "Arrest, Trial, Prison, Murdered in Prison" – and the full story unfolds in all its delightfully blunt glory.

While undoubtedly not a new medium of expression, the single-panel narrative has largely been confined to magazines, newspapers and book illustrations – where, often, a line from the text is taken as a starting point for an accompanying artwork. Many comic-book artists, however, are keen to play with the constructs (and confines) of their medium, often resorting to a single panel to convey an implied narrative.

US artist Jim Woodring believes that the reader, on encountering his highly detailed single-panel works, will naturally go through the following stages: "1) Observing the seemingly discordant composition and the irksome need to look at the details instead of the whole. 2) Scrutinizing the picture's details and initially finding them to be chaotic and unrelated. 3) Noticing that there are connections between the details after all, and that by letting the eye travel from one detail to another one sees relationships between and among them. 4) Seeing that the composition is not random, and that the configuration of the rooms and framing elements provide a cohesive frame of reference for the middle ground events. 5) Beginning to recognize that there is a story in the picture and beginning to 'read' that story. 6) Examining all the elements to see if they are all part of a plan or just a bunch of hooey. 7) Rejecting the hooey theory. 8) Reading the story. 9) And so to bed."

Paul Davis' story Clint Flick (included here on pages 46–49) is typical of his trademark single-panel narratives. However, this particular unpublished project from the UK illustrator shows how the form can be both a series of individual panels and a whole sequenced narrative. In this sense, Davis's skill lies in being able to create four autonomous pieces that can also form part of a larger story when placed together.

Taking Salman Rushdie's epic novel Midnight's Children as her inspiration, Bhushan created a series of ten images while studying at the Royal College of Art in London. The series won first prize in the 2003 Folio Society's book illustration competition. "I think that my work has a quiet intensity and a narrative quality which reflects my interest in storytelling, fiction and the process of reading," she says. "I love the fact that words on a page are silent and yet create a whole sensory world in your brain which is noisy and lively and full of images."

Miss Forbes's Summer of Happiness, 2001

I Only Came to Use the Phone, 2000

Inspired by Gabriel García Marquez's book Strange Pilgrims, these haunting examples of Bhushan's personal work were also completed while she was studying at the Royal College of Art in London.

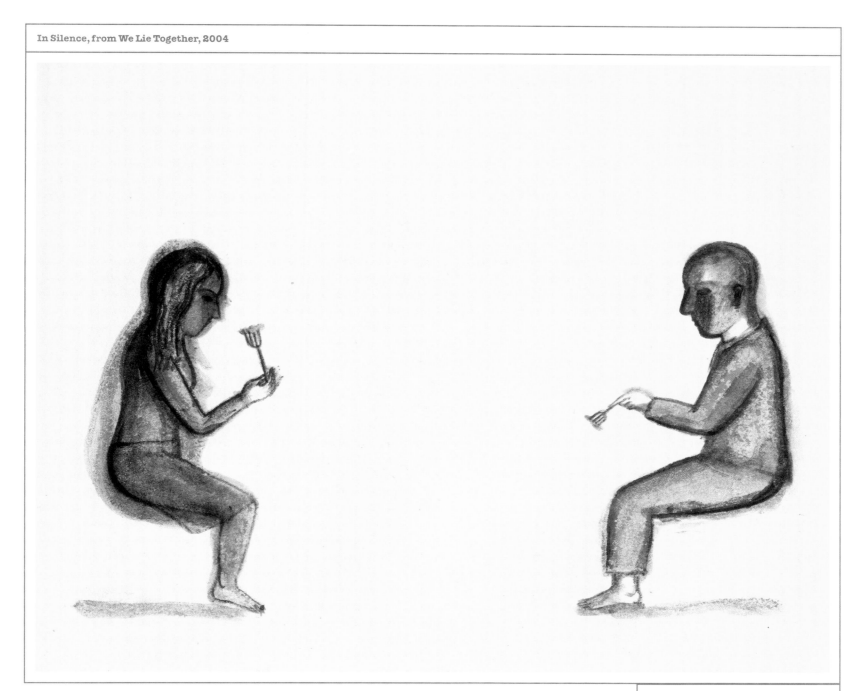

This heavily emotive image forms a spread from the book We Lie Together, which Bhushan wrote with fellow Royal College of Art graduate Laura Carlin. "The idea was to create a book within a book," explains Bhushan, "a book in two layers. When you first read it, you see Laura's images that show an idyllic domestic environment, with the words enhancing this. As the book is French-folded, after reading it through, the reader then tears open the pages along the folds to reveal my images within and the meaning of the story is inverted."

Who's Still Out There

Chémical Ali

Dr. Germ

Mrs. Anthrax

Captain Cholesterol

Grandma Mold

Ayatollah Ebola

Mr. Second-hand Smoke

Video Poker Kamel

Professor Asbestos

Lieutenant Sloth

Ultra-violet Tariq

Reality TV Achmed

Commander Caffeine

Major Stress

Presidential Allergies (right) was one of the first cartoons that US-based illustrator Barry Blitt had published by the New Yorker magazine. Explains Blitt: "I just drew it to amuse myself, it doesn't mean a damn thing, and Françoise Mouly, who was just starting as art editor there, took it and asked for more… Who's Still Out There [left], also for the New Yorker, was another case where the Iraq War was in all our faces, it was just a reaction to the comical names of some of the 'villains'." Although Blitt says that the New Yorker will occasionally ask for comic art tied to a specific news story or seasonal event, he rarely agrees to work to a brief. Welcome to Egypt (far right) is a personal piece created while on holiday in Sinai, Egypt. "I bring pen and ink wherever I go, so I can draw if I get an idea or want to isolate myself from people."

Presidential Allergies, 1994

Welcome to Egypt, 1999

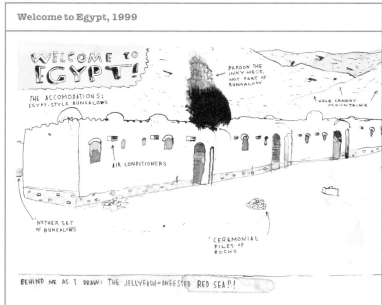

Drawn by London-based illustrator Paul Davis, these four illustrations were originally commissioned by designer Gerard Saint, of London studio Big Active, for a book project about swearing. Sadly the publisher folded before the book was printed and these images have remained unpublished until now. Each piece was drawn by hand before then being scanned and coloured on a Mac.

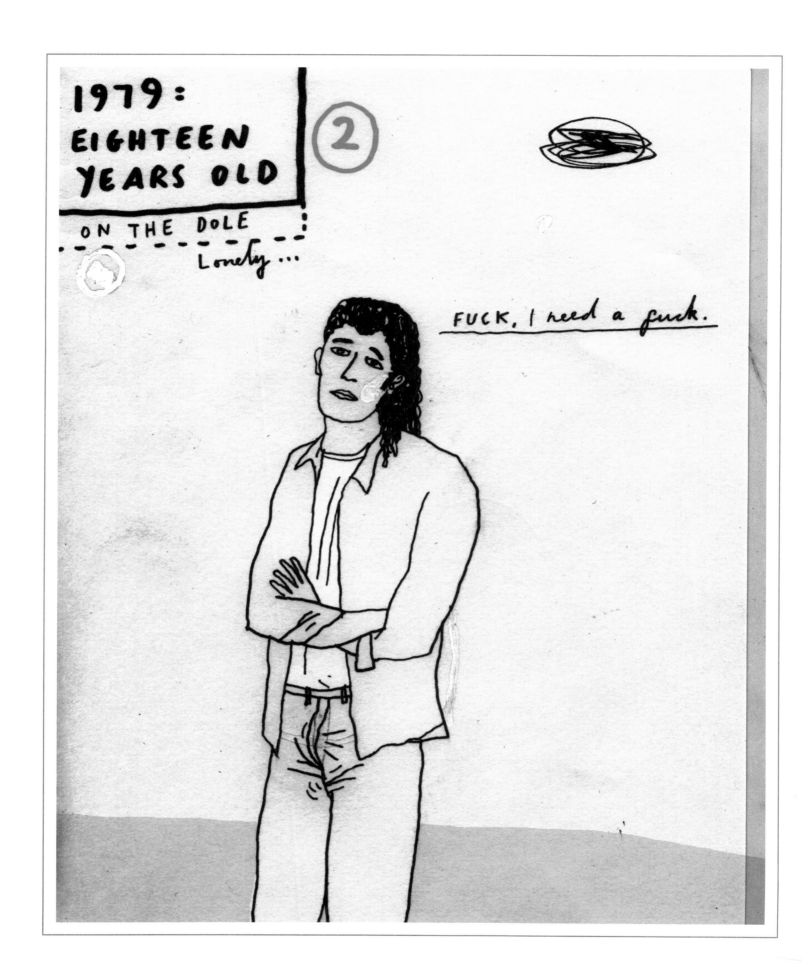

Marcel Dzama

Dzama employs a host of bizarre characters in his delicate drawings and paintings, depicting surreal situations in which tree-people ride bikes and strangely mutated children exist alongside normally proportioned adults. In examples like these, Dzama simply lets his drawn worlds speak for themselves.
The black and white pages featured overleaf appeared as Marcel Dzama's Super Happy Fun Comic Page in the second issue of the UK comics anthology Sturgeon White Moss. The images used on this spread are courtesy of David Zwirner, New York.

A Prospective Scene in Winnipeg, 2004

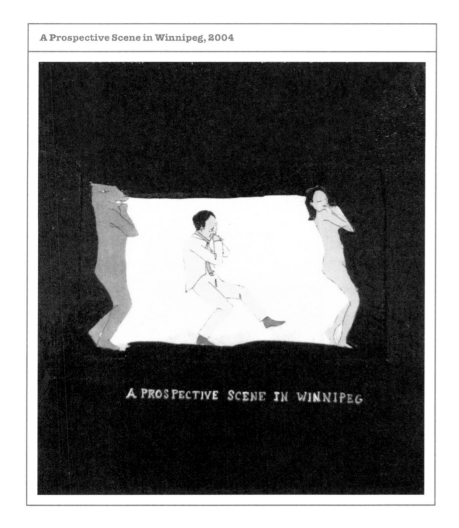

Untitled, 2004

Published weekly in the Independent on Sunday newspaper, this series of single-panel illustrations was created by illustrator Scott Garrett. There have been over 150 to date; the first, entitled No More Mr Nice Guy, was published in June 2001. Garrett explains: "I was commissioned to start a series on the strength of my personal sketchbooks, which were similar in feel to these illustrations. The Independent on Sunday wanted someone who could do something that wasn't too obscure but was amusing in a more obvious way. David Shrigley had preceded me, with Peter Blegvad before him. They already had a Glenn Baxter panel." These pieces are created in pencil and watercolour on sugar paper. Garrett says the ideas "are triggered by things I see or hear in everyday life, or they start with an image or character I'd like to work with. Like a penguin."

from ?, 2003

WHAT DID YOU HAVE FOR LUNCH?

WHAT'S YOUR DOG'S NAME ?

WHERE ARE YOU GOING?

HOW DO YOU FEEL?

CAN YOU SPEAK FREN-CH?

WHERE WERE YOU BORN?

Tom Gauld

All six single panels shown here are taken from Gauld's comic entitled ?, published as part of his Three Very Small Comics (three comics published together and presented in an envelope). "I drew each of these comics in a day," says Gauld. "They're just simple, silly ideas; each comic is printed on one side of an A4 sheet of paper and folded up in a special way to make a tiny, eight-page book." Of the inspiration behind ?, Gauld adds: "I don't know where the idea for asking these weird people questions came from, and there's no real meaning to it, it just seemed funny to ask them banal questions. The drawings were done quickly on scraps of paper and without any pencilling or preparation, which is unusual for me."

Artist and illustrator Simone Lia dedicates most of her time to creating her own comic books, which are published by Cabanon Press, the imprint that Lia founded with Tom Gauld. Poor Bloody Victor is a personal series drawn in ink on paper. The inspiration, Lia tells us, "came from some old work colleagues who would always refer to someone they knew as 'poor bloody Victor.'" "I never did meet Victor," she adds, "but I drew some unpleasant scenarios to suit his name."

The Chip and Bean panels were initially drawn by hand and then completed on a computer. Though Chip and Bean first appeared in Lia and Gauld's comic entitled First, the images shown here were created in 2004 and screenprinted as postcards.

Says Lia of the ongoing series: "The Chip and Bean characters have a loving relationship but I think it is also quite unhealthy. They live in their own world and they find beauty and happiness in things that other people would find ugly or annoying. Bean is dominant and Chip is mute."

Snap Out of It, drawn in ink on paper, first appeared in Second, a comic Lia put together with Tom Gauld. Fluffy is a graphic novel published in four parts and tells the story of a man and his bunny and their trip to Sicily (see pages 102–3). Each chapter apparently takes about six months to complete. Shown here is one of the illustrations of a musical therapist created for page breaks throughout.

Drawn while still at the Royal College of Art in London, this piece is, says Mills, "an interrupted narrative, a point of departure, an appropriated scene, a missing element, an absence."

G

Gone With

LIVERPOOL JOHN MOORES UNIVERSITY
LEARNING SERVICES

Pantophobia, 2003

Necromorphous, 2003

Created to illustrate the entry for "necromorphous" in The Superior Person's Second Book of Words by Peter Bowler (published by Bloomsbury), the meaning of this strange word – "Feigning death to deter an aggressor" – is conveyed in Mills's scrappy, freeform style (right). Mills applied the same spontaneous approach to his interpretation of the all-encompassing word "Pantophobia" – the "morbid fear of everything" (above).

Disapproval, 2004

For the back cover of the book
How to Be Idle by Tom Hodgkinson
(published by Penguin), Mills
created an illustration that
effortlessly implied a sense of not
only the book's title, but the name of
his own amusing drawing as well.

Another awkward and deliberately messy drawing by artist David Shrigley that celebrates the various ups and downs of life.

With all its domestic and homely details, this image of the interior of a space station sailing through the silence of deep space may be part of, Wightman believes, "an attempt to humanize space exploration with all the dirty washing and whatnot". Here the reader can construct a narrative of the day-to-day running of the station by reading the rooms as panels. The image of a large building or an architectural structure such as this lends itself particularly well to this kind of narrative construction and a single drawn page or panel can be divided into smaller panels, following the structure of the building itself.

Jim Woodring

Both of these single-panel narratives are intended to be examined closely. According to Woodring, who is concentrating on working in this way instead of his usual comic-book form, they are "pictures that forego traditional pictorial composition in order to be read as stories". They are part of Woodring's thematically similar paintings and charcoal works which are included in his collection Seeing Things, published by Fantagraphics.

If this stand-alone work has the intended effect, the viewer should go through the stages described in the introduction to this section: from scrutinizing the details in the frame, noticing the connections between what is, at first glance, a discordant composition, to finally being able to "read" the story.

In this section we explore how contemporary narrative illustrators and comics artists adopt different approaches to the juxtaposition of text and image in forming their narratives. While it can be argued that the eighteenth- and nineteenth-century satirists Thomas Rowlandson and James Gillray are the fathers of the speech balloon, this concept was around long before either artist was born. Some artists were adopting bands of text within their artworks as early as the fifteenth century. These bands, which are sometimes referred to as speech bands, flags or scrolls, developed into our modern-day speech balloons over the years and by the early seventeenth century the speech was actually coming directly from the mouth of the person speaking, albeit still in band form. While Gillray's work tended more to the single-panel format, Rowlandson combined many ideas that are common today. Making use of both speech and thought balloons, he also used a fully developed frame format, with some frames larger than others to allow enough space for all the details.

This traditional formula is one used by contemporary artists such as Simone Lia, Tom Gauld, Jordan Crane, Martin tom Dieck, Igort, Barnaby Richards, Jenni Rope, Joe Sacco and Jason, though some of these also employ sound effects in their work. Marjane Satrapi also adopts these methods, but develops the medium further in her story Persepolis by taking speech out of a balloon when she wants to convey that the main character is shouting. In his comic Black Death, Sammy Harkham only uses speech, presented in balloons, once the action is static; movement therefore is depicted by silence. Benoît Jacques takes the idea further still by including both caption and speech-balloon text in his Comique Trip, which is written entirely in Chinese script. This is to hint implicitly at a verbal storyline and is Jacques's attempt to take a sideways look at the connection between text and drawings.

Despite the influence of Rowlandson and Gillray, however, it is widely accepted that the first modern example of a speech balloon appeared in American artist Richard Fenton Outcalt's The Yellow Kid. First published in 1896 in the New York World, this also marked the birth of the comic genre in the American press. The Yellow Kid resulted in an immediate increase in the World's circulation and arguably paved the way for succeeding comic strips, though it is important not to forget the importance of an even earlier work, this time created by Swiss artist Rudolph Töpffer in 1837 and only recently rediscovered in California (in 1998). The Adventures of Obadiah Oldbuck, a 40-page side-stitched comic book, was made up of six to 12 panels per page and each illustration was captioned with text beneath the panels to describe the story.

Reminiscent of this style is the work showcased in the following pages by both Jeff Fisher, whose beautiful illustrations are accompanied by a line of typography, and Fredrik von Blixen, whose two comics, Lost and Found, read more like an illustrated poem, with the final interpretation of their meaning being left to the reader.

Of course, these boundaries and rules can be pushed and the examples of Jochen Gerner's work featured here were chosen precisely for this reason. In TNT en Amérique, Gerner paints over an existing Tintin comic to uncover an entirely new form of narrative, while his En Ligne(s) drawings depict a chaotic stream of consciousness out of which recurring themes emerge. David Rees, by contrast, uses clip art found on the internet as a vehicle for his dialogue and social commentary, explaining: "Clip art is a good way to introduce the art of comic narrative to people who might otherwise be intimidated by a perceived lack of artist talent. It usually serves a strictly utilitarian purpose, and its anonymous, often uncopyrighted nature is an intriguing contrast to other types of art. It can serve as the impersonal structural units through which more creative personal art is produced."

Text and Image 👉

Fredrik von Blixen **p69**
Jordan Crane **p72**
Martin tom Dieck **p74**
Jeff Fisher **p76**
Tom Gauld **p78**
Jochen Gerner **p82**
Sammy Harkham **p88**
Igort **p92**
Benoît Jacques **p96**
Jason **p100**
Simone Lia **p102**
Lorenzo Mattotti **p105**
David Rees **p108**
Barnaby Richards **p110**
Jenni Rope **p114**
Joe Sacco **p117**
Marjane Satrapi **p121**
David Shrigley **p125**
Singh & Dunning **p128**
Katja Tukiainen **p130**

Von Blixen's story of losing and finding reads like an illustrated poem, with the delicate ink drawings adding another dimension of mystery to the dreamlike text. Lost is the second, Found the final part of a trilogy that still awaits a first instalment. The reader is left to contemplate the combined effect of image and text which does not necessarily point to answers or arrive at conclusions. The effect, rather, is more impressionistic and relies on personal interpretation. "It began as an intention to conclude what my notion of 'lost' is," says von Blixen. "However, I'm still looking for it and the moral of the story changes every time I flick through its pages. I suppose I lost my head and found a box of 'ifs' and 'ors' that will never stop bothering me."

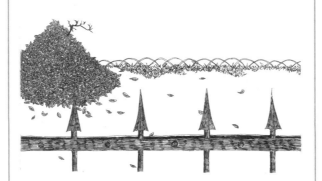

When dealing with something completely lost... one must assume it is in hiding.

Looking for it requires patience, and somewhat of a vague feeling.

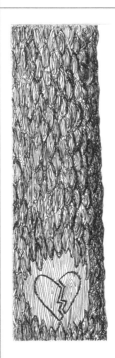

Committing to the search is paramount, or the trail of thought is lost...

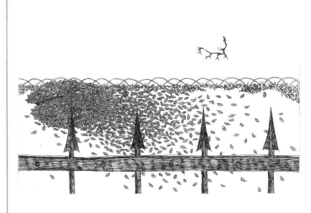

...and one must start from the top.

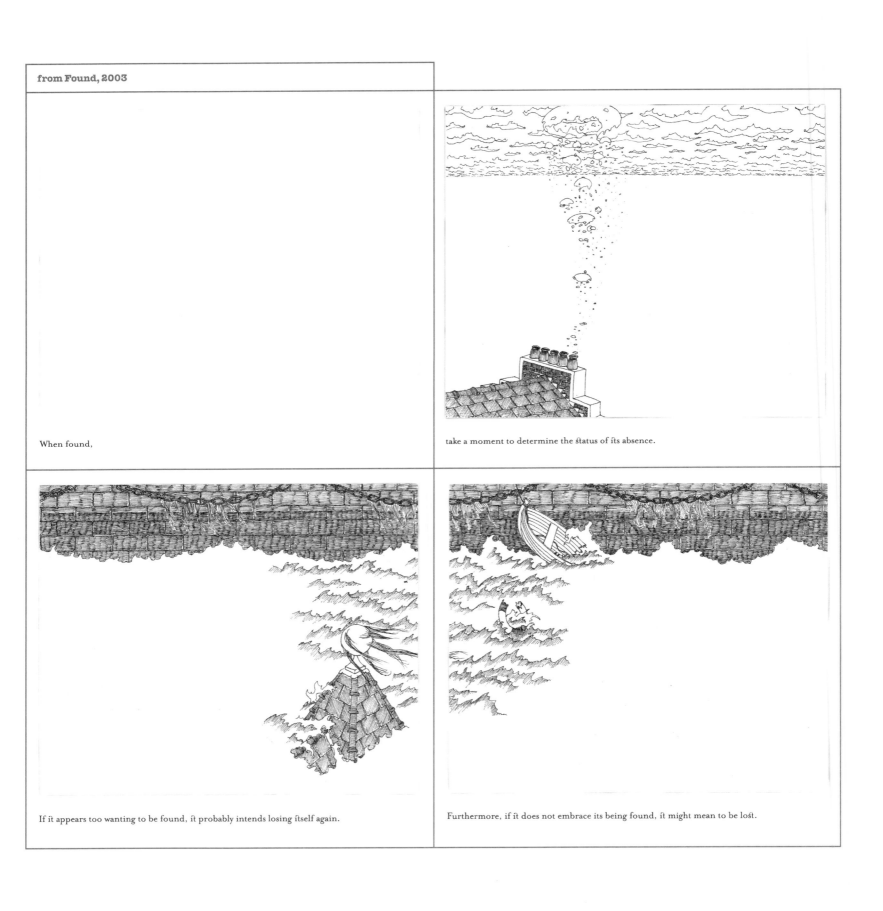

When found,

take a moment to determine the status of its absence.

If it appears too wanting to be found, it probably intends losing itself again.

Furthermore, if it does not embrace its being found, it might mean to be lost.

The status will reveal its motive.

However, whatever you do, never ask the subject of is object…

…because something absent is in no condition to reflect on its state.

Disreguard its sweet words and best of intentions, as they are all lies.

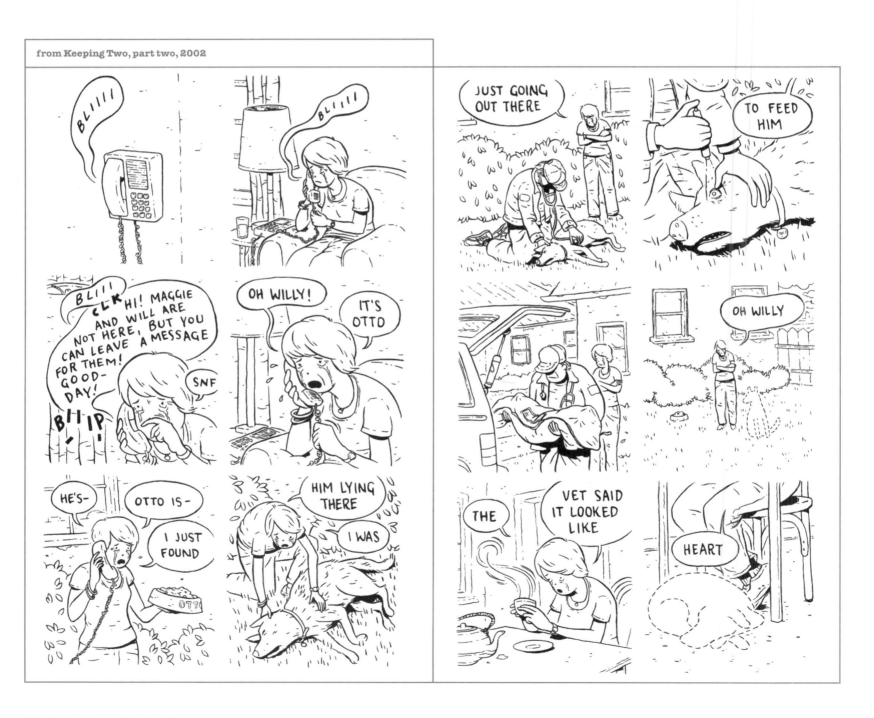

Jordan Crane

This sequence shows Crane's skill in conveying a story within a story. In the second part of his Keeping Two series, Crane displays visually the contents of a message that the mother of the main character, Will, has left on his answering machine. Will's mother's dog has died and Crane gives the spoken message over images of the scenes described.

The undefined edges of each panel indicate a past event and the speaker's jerky, tearful retelling is reflected in the panels' layout – each word is punctuated between the panels as she struggles to get the story out. The outlined shape of the dog also hints at the void now present, linking back to the baby lost by the couple in the earlier part of the story (see pages 14–15). The comic is about what it feels like to lose someone and imagining the pain of loss itself – something that is passed on to the reader.

Martin tom Dieck

This dreamlike 14-page story was published in book form in German by Reprodukt in 2001, having previously appeared in Die Zeit magazine. "In each issue there was a strip with three images – the content was completely up to me," says tom Dieck. Shown here are the final eight panels of the sequence, which was, he explains, "built around the moment between sleeping and waking and the attempt to make this moment lasting."

The German text in the fourth panel translates as "Alas, those old songs," while the seventh panel reads: "What, however, do we know under water?" In the strip, the main character is depicted gathering up all of his smaller "selves" from his bedroom floor while in a hypnogogic state.

Shown here is work by artist Jeff Fisher taken from his book How to Get Rich, published by Bloomsbury in 2001. Throughout the book, the illustrations are either shown on a single page or double-page spread and each is accompanied by a caption. Although each illustration stands as an artwork in its own right, together they form an underlying narrative that explores, in Fisher's words, "the hopelessness of becoming rich".

YOU ATTEMPT A MODEST LIVING BY HARD WORK, DECENCY, FRUGALITY, AND INTEGRITY

YOU HANDSTITCH TINY PARTS OF PIECES OF RUBBISH TO OTHER BITS

YOU PUSH YOURSELF BEYOND THE LIMITS OF HUMAN ENDURANCE

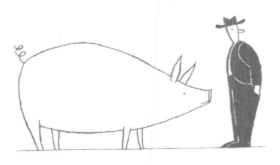

YOU BUY PIG FUTURES

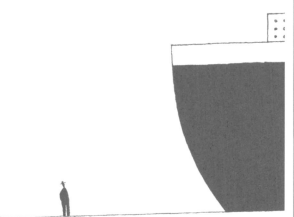

YOUR BOAT
COMES IN

YOUR BOAT
GOES OUT

A MULTITUDE OF SMALL CREATURES CARRIES YOU OFF TO THE LAND BEYOND THE CLOUDS WHERE YOU ARE DECLARED KING OF HEAVEN, FED FRESH FISH, CHOCOLATE CAKE & AS MUCH WINE AS YOU CAN DRINK.......

Despite Guardians of the Kingdom's billing as an epic tale of adventure and romance, the two rather bored guards who patrol the walls of the kingdom encounter very little of either. Gauld's deft control of language and dialogue creates a clever situation in which the stark and dramatic landscapes are peppered with the mundane chatter of two characters seemingly waiting for something to happen.

Commissioned for London's Time Out magazine, Move to the City featured the weekly adventures of, says Gauld, "two country-bumpkin types walking along a road to a city, where not much happened, and they only got there in the final episode. I hoped that the readers would become quite attached to the two innocent, idiotic characters and worry about how they'd fare when they got to the big city, as represented by the rest of Time Out." The measured pace of the action reflected the gradual unfolding of the narrative through the dialogue between the two characters. Gauld explains: "It was intended as a slow, calm respite from the relentless hipness and activity in the magazine and city."

As part of a series for the Guardian newspaper's Saturday Review section, Gauld produced several strips about famous literary figures. "None of the writers did any writing, they just had banal everyday experiences," says Gauld of the strips which captured the solitude of the writer's profession and some of the mundane events that may have distracted its practitioners from their work. His strips adopted a similar structure over the seven weeks that Writers at Work ran.

Part of the second volume of Very Small Comics, published through his and Simone Lia's imprint Cabanon Press, Gauld's Invasion is about a soldier landing on an island inhabited by only one man and several sheep. "The soldier claims the land for his king and country," says Gauld, "but the shepherd isn't too bothered and they both get along quite well."

Published by L'Ampoule in 2002, French designer and illustrator Jochen Gerner's book TNT en Amérique takes Hergé's famous Tintin en Amérique comic book as its starting point. Interested by the theme of violence and American society, Gerner bought old copies of the comic and painted the pages black, leaving only selected words visible (although, for copyright reasons, the words then had to be rewritten by Gerner himself).

Slowly the pages started to look like a night scene with spots of colour where he allowed signs, pictograms and symbols to "appear like little urban lights, like flashing pop neon lighting in the violent obscurity of the American city".
"I treat the theme of violence," he continues, "but also the notions of noise, of movement, of money, of religion, of Good and Evil that go with it."

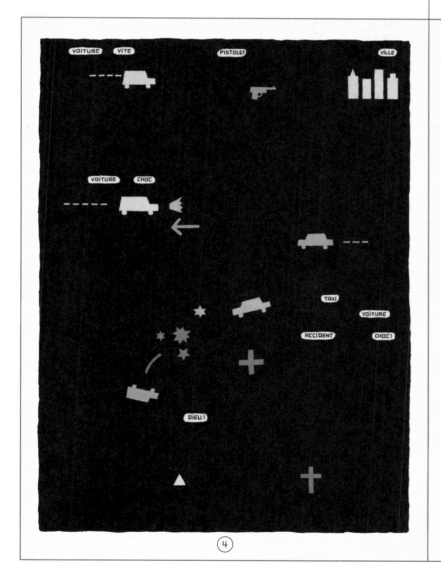

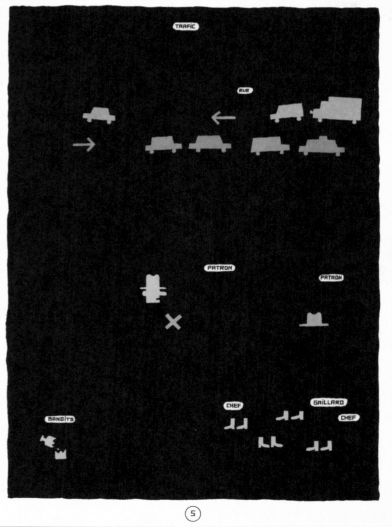

En Ligne(s) is a replica of a notebook of doodles and messages created by Gerner while talking on the telephone between 1994 and 2002.

When a friend suggested that he publish the work, Gerner simply added introductory texts to explain his thought processes and listed the recurring graphic elements. The final version was published by L'Ampoule in 2003.

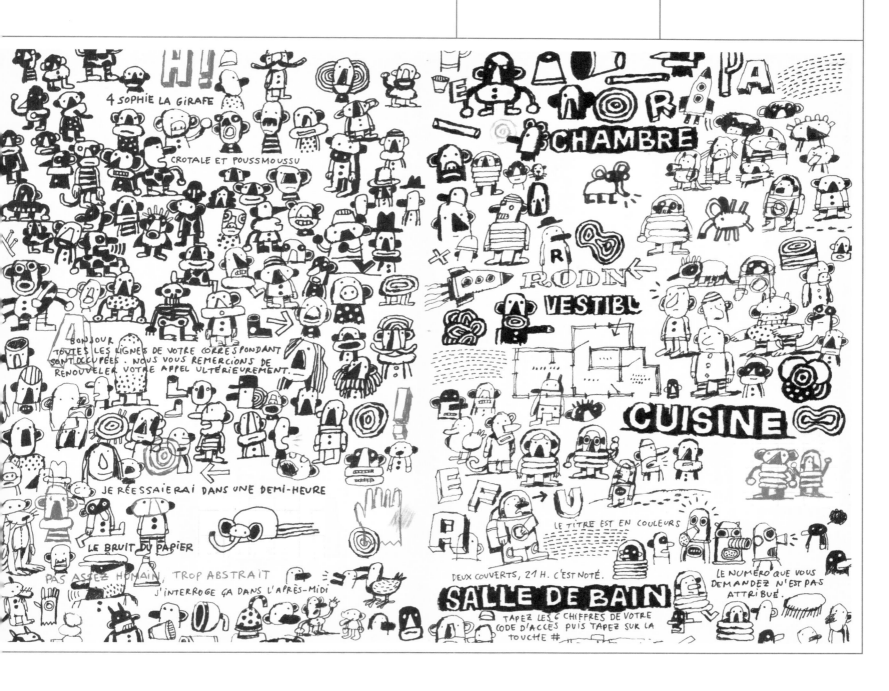

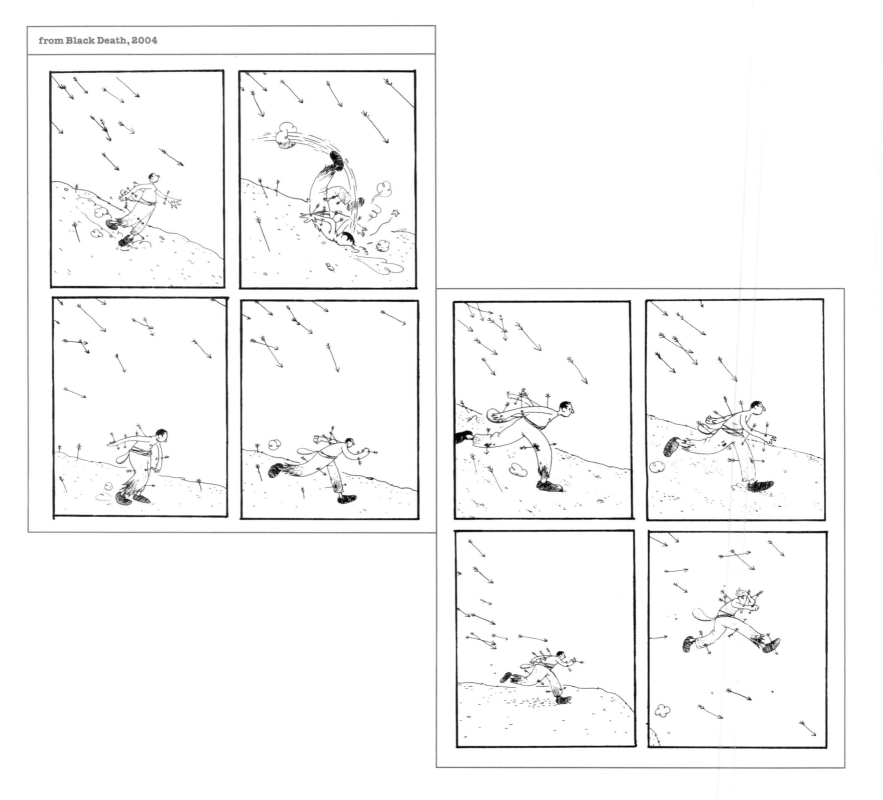

The great sense of movement and momentum in the opening pages of Harkham's Black Death is cleverly conveyed silently – the main character's first words only appear in response to his predicament when he finally comes to standstill. "Black Death comes out of a desire to see good genre fiction in comics," says Harkham. "Hopefully, it'll have all the things I like in 'serious' fiction, like complex characters, subtlety, depth, etc, and have the best things from genre fiction, like a certain level of mystery, fun and excitement, with space to explore things like myth and folklore. Black Death is a space for all that to exist."

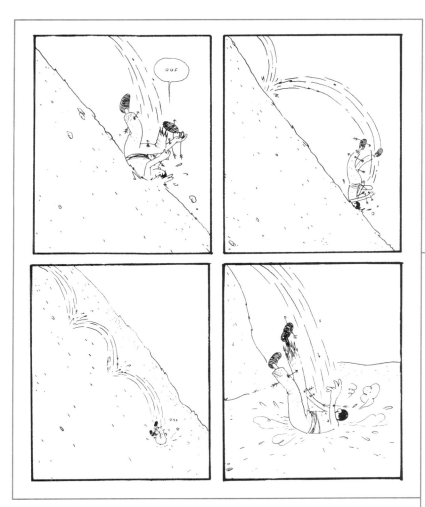

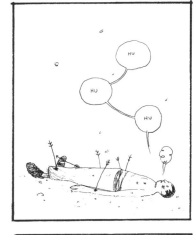

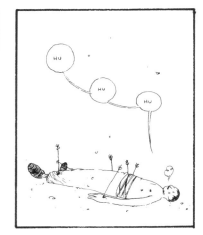

At the other end of the spectrum from the more considered and draughtsmanlike approach to creating comic narratives, Harkham's short story Alexander the Greatest is almost a stream-of-consciousness piece, the form echoing the nature of the narrative. "I just sat down and drew it and let it become as subjective as possible and ramble off to wherever seemed right," he says of the creative process involved. "Usually when working on a story I try to create some distance from the characters so that the reader can feel a certain level of objectivity. This strip was the exact opposite to everything I had tried to do before. Formally, I wanted the page to physically resemble the dreamlike nature of the story."

This story was inspired by La Bohème, the famous opera by Giacomo Puccini, and is set in Paris at the height of the Jazz Age. "It's about the poverty among artists, about friendship, about some strange things asked of a musician," says Igort. "If you read the lyrics of the opera you will find a lot of similarities. But I put all this into the style of gangster stories."

Paris   "Come on, we've got to celebrate."   "Women, more women and wine!"   How can it be so cold when spring has already begun.

QUANDO LO VIDE
PENSAVA A SUA FIGLIA,

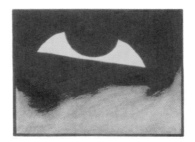

E A SUA MOGLIE CHE
SE NE ERA ANDATA
CON IL BATTERISTA.

TUTTI SANNO QUANTO
POSSONO ESSERE
CRUDELI GLI UCCELLI.

When he saw it, he was thinking of his daughter, and his wife, who had gone off with the drummer. We all know how cruel birds can be.

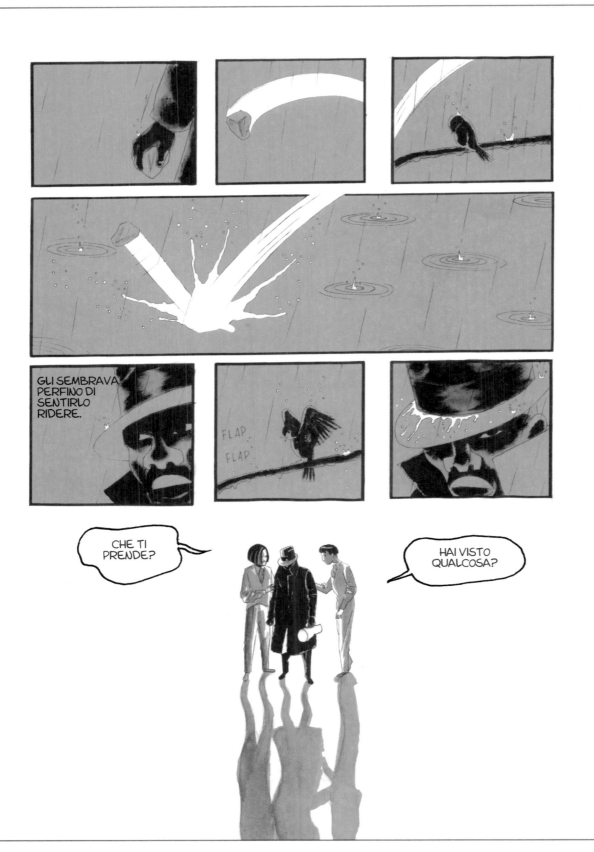

It was as though he could   "What's up with you?"   "Did you see something?"
hear it laughing.

In this scene from Caruso, one of the main characters, Peppino, is transported to memories of his father through playing his Caruso records and breathing in the smell of his brand of hair cream.

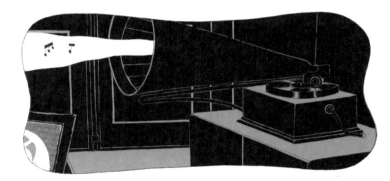

In the days leading up to the funeral, while the women were crying, he locked himself into the lounge of that big house to listen to Caruso's records.

His aunt Silvana was not happy about music being played on days of mourning; she told him off, but Peppino was a stubborn little boy. (Knock knock) "Open this blasted door! Peppino…" "Open it!" Caruso kept on singing.

He would close the shutters and turn off the lights. Once in the dark, when he was sure nobody could see him, he would open the tin of hair cream and breathe in deeply.

It was then that the magic occurred. That penetrating smell almost made him feel like he was with his father.

In his first incursion into comic books, the self-published Comique Trip, Jacques demonstrated his ability to convey a narrative through signs and characters, such as financial data, Chinese letters (shown here) or picture symbols (shown overleaf). "I like comics because I'm interested in the connection between text and drawings," he says. "I get annoyed by the way this language can become stereotyped, though, and while there are plenty of fantastic artists that use this medium to experiment and produce great things, this was an attempt to look at this sideways." Jacques used materials such as cuttings from magazines and old books alongside his drawings to convey a narrative progression. "A bit like the Surrealists might have done," he says, "I invent a visual story."

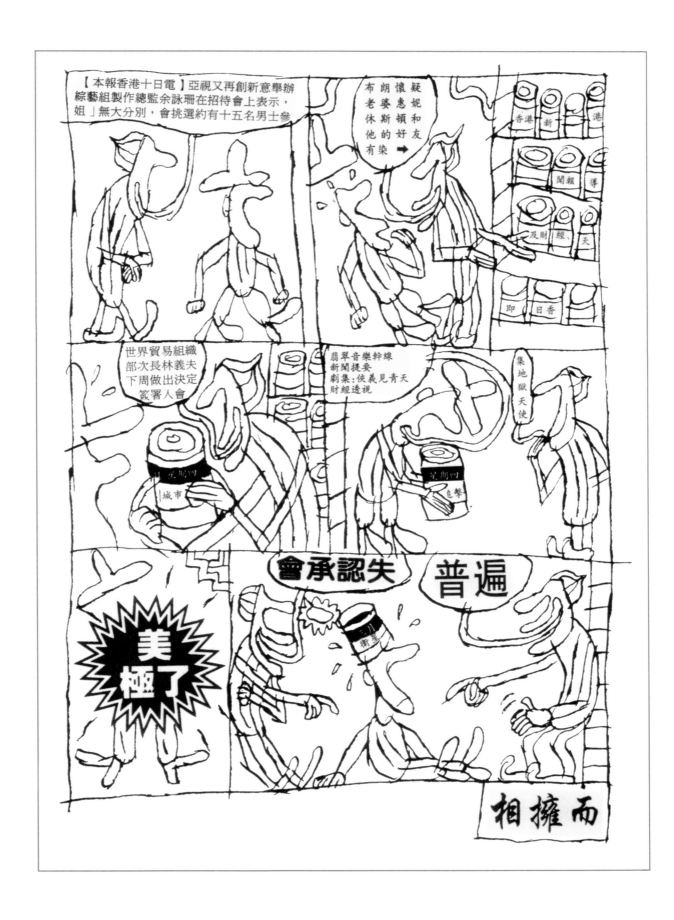

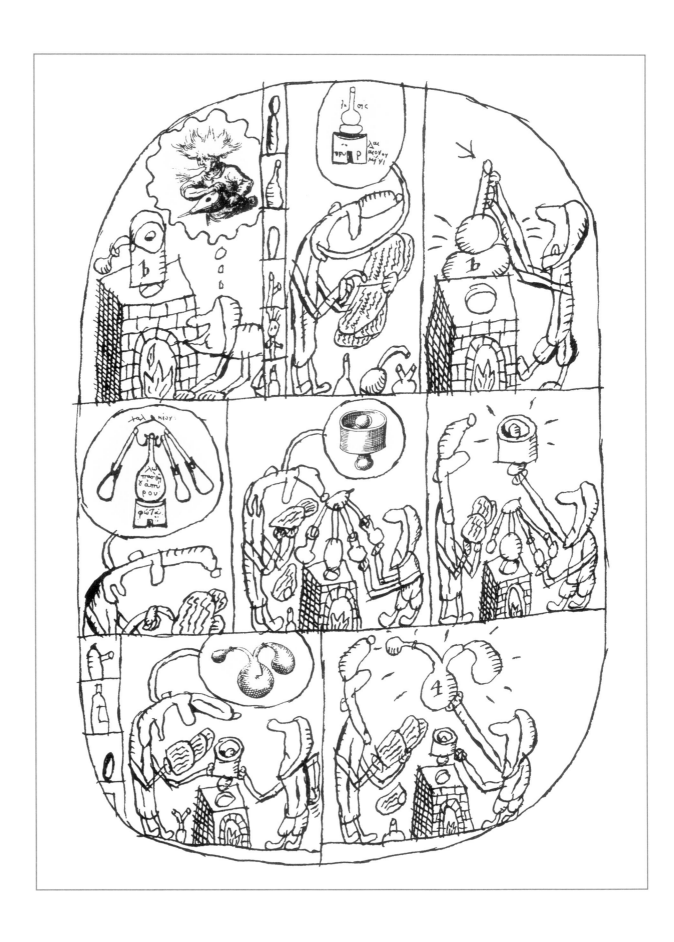

Jason

The novel Jernvognen (The Iron Wagon), a murder mystery set in and around a rural hotel in Hvaler, near Oslo, was written by Norwegian crime writer Stein Riverton and published in Norway in 1909. For his retelling of the story in graphic form, Jason used a minimal palette of black, white and red. "I heard a radio play version of The Iron Wagon when I was about 15 years old, and was struck by the haunting atmosphere of the story," he says. "I read the novel and almost immediately started seeing images in my head, thinking about how it could be told as a comic book. It was then a matter of waiting until I felt I could do the story justice, and it actually took almost 20 years."

Fluffy is a graphic novel published in four parts that tells the story of a man and his bunny and their trip to Sicily. Part one was published in the summer of 2003, part two in August 2004, while this year will see the appearance of the final two instalments.

LIVERPOOL JOHN MOORES UNIVERSITY
LEARNING SERVICES

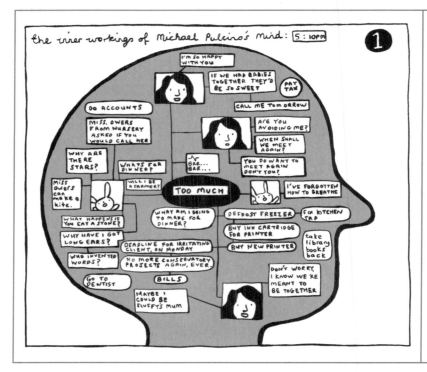

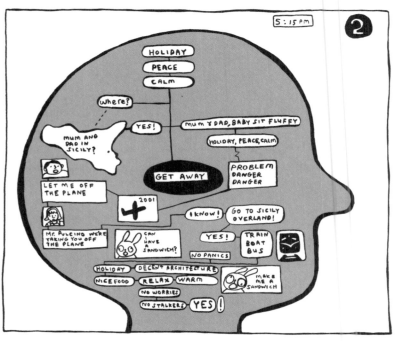

Italian fine artist and narrative illustrator Lorenzo Mattotti, today based in Paris, combines the use of pencil and pastels to produce the striking panels of rich vibrant colours and fluid lines that make up the comic books which he creates in conjunction with different writers. Examples shown here are taken from: Bruit du Givre (Sound of Frost), written by Jorge Zentner and published by Le Seuil in 2003. This story tells the tale of one man's soul-searching journey to find his estranged ex. Labyrinthes, a collection of ten dream-based stories, was written by Jerry Kramsky and published by Le Seuil in 1999. Caboto was again written by Jorge Zentner and published by Le Seuil in 2003.

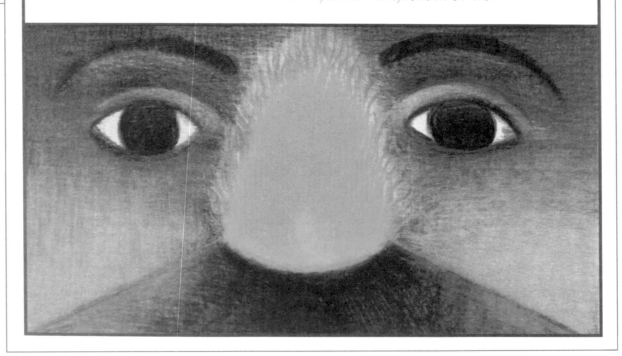

Alice's letter arrived from a country far away, very far away. I went to find an atlas…

… as if it were possible to find again the smell of her skin on maps.

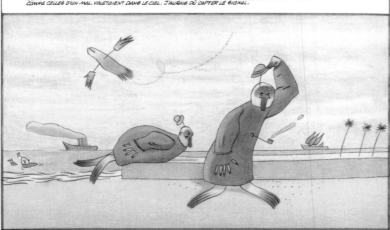

I came across some gentlemen swimmers on the beach.
They promised to help me with their advice.
Believing falsely that I could find my grandfather easily,
I let the shaman go. Inconsiderate threats fluttered in
the sky like those of a pain. I should have got the message.

Following the swimmers' directions,
I headed into the salubrious alleys
behind the door of memories.
None of these degenerate creatures
could be him.

I ended up in the rubbish room, where
pathetic characters had been left.
With each trumpeting, the animals
left on the junk heap lost all dignity.
What then could they reveal to me?

Until another bureaucrat informed me
that my permit to prowl these parts had
expired. I could only have remained as
an accidental part of the furnishings.

I could not be sure of my direct
influence but when the tempest was
over, an enormous narwhal had
appeared in the paddy fields
surrounding the farmers' houses.

So I returned to our world with a few
ritual decorations and a crazy idea:
as I couldn't find him in death, I would
bring my grandfather back to life.
A storm broke.

The noble mammal was about to die.
His final look was one of reproach!
What if it had been one of my
grandfather's 10,000 possible
reincarnations?

A caravel and a brig, loaded with ambitions and dreams, invent, in their distractions, uncertain future itineraries.

Commanding these two ships is Caboto: trader, navigator, scientist, a man used to dealing with kings and cabin boys, bankers, soldiers, cartographers, a man of complex ambition.

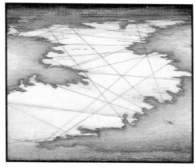

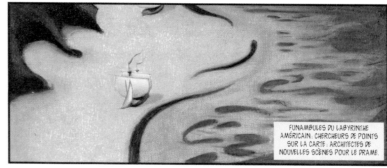

Tightrope walkers of the American labyrinth: seekers of places on maps: architects of new sets for the drama.

David Rees

New York-based David Rees creates his comic strips by adding his own words to clip art found free on the internet. Having first developed this technique for a series entitled My New Fighting Technique Is Unstoppable, a comic collection that features clip-art karate masters, Rees went on to produce a sequel, My New Filing Technique Is Unstoppable, this time featuring open-plan office employees talking on the telephone.

It was in October 2001, shortly after 9/11, that Rees began posting Get Your War On. His cubicle employees now really had something to talk about.

While the strips shown here were initially posted on Rees's website at www.mnftiu.cc, they have since been collected in two anthologies: Get Your War On (Soft Skull Press, 2002) and Get Your War On II (Riverhead Books, 2004).

from Get Your War On, 2002

While studying medieval art at university, Richards became fascinated by church iconography and architecture, particularly the context within which certain symbols appeared – gargoyles, for example, have a practical use (as drainpipes) as well as a symbolic function. "Somehow this brings them to life, because you give them a day-to-day reason for being," says Richards. "I try to make my characters work in the same way." Of his character Sawbird, who distributes the mail in his short comic Art & Agatha, Richards states simply, "He is what he is and you can see him for yourself. It constantly baffles me that people want a preconceived explanation for things. Walking down the street, you don't ask a stranger you see to explain themselves, you interpret their behaviour for yourself." Richards is a firm believer in comics existing as parallel worlds with their own internal logic. "Comics picture the appearance of things," he says, "and however unlikely that appearance is, they try to breathe life into it. It's a form of alchemy."

Despite the hand-crafted feel and medieval look of the characters and settings in The Funeral, Richards's small comic published by Atlantic Press, the tale itself – of loss and return – was actually inspired by a more modern aspect of contemporary life. "Not that long ago I lost my mobile phone," Richards explains. "I had no other record of all my contacts and so had no way of getting in touch with anyone. This is what The Funeral is about: being taken out of the equation but at the same time still being present. All the hairiness is inspired by the wildmen and women that often inhabit the margins of medieval art."

Finnish artist, illustrator and designer Jenni Rope's comic book Monday, published under her own Napa Books imprint in 2002, tells the story of a day in the life of a lonely man. The comic was first hand-drawn in pencil before Rope added textures using Freehand software.

"Inspiration comes from my own life and dreams," explains Rope. "I use things that have a strange meaning to me, things that I happen to draw a lot like tables, legs and wine glasses. I also collect strange moments, then sew them together to make a story. I try to recreate the feeling and the atmosphere of little everyday moments." Rope has since also created comics called Tuesday, Wednesday and Thursday in a continuation of her Weekday series.

from Monday, 2002

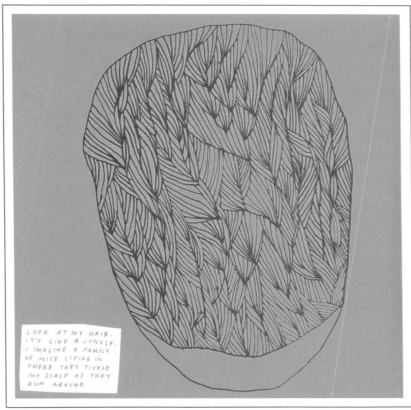

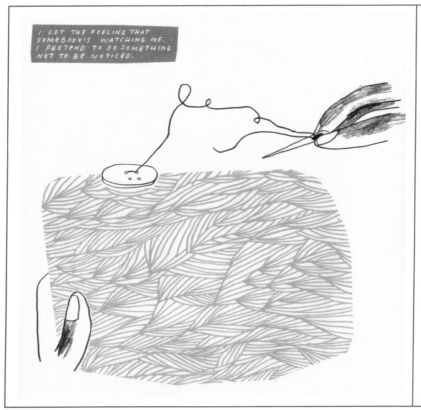

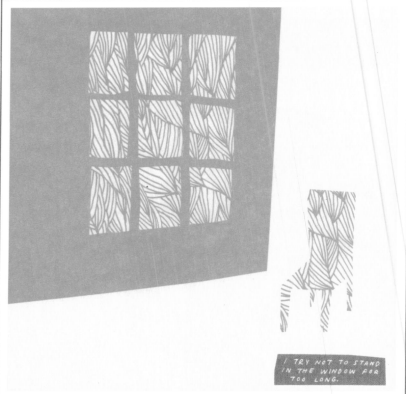

As a journalist recording his time in post-war Sarajevo in 1995, Sacco met Neven, a "fixer". Neven's role as a fixer was to lead Western reporters to the tragic human stories that occurred during the disintegration of civil order in Bosnia. Sacco charts how journalists often relied on these shadowy people in order to obtain information on the warlords and gangsters who retained a tight grip on the devastated country. This extract, from the beginning of Sacco's retelling of his first meetings with Neven, conveys the secrecy of their dealings. Through tight captioning and a sparse narration, Sacco immediately creates a claustrophobic and unpredictable atmosphere.

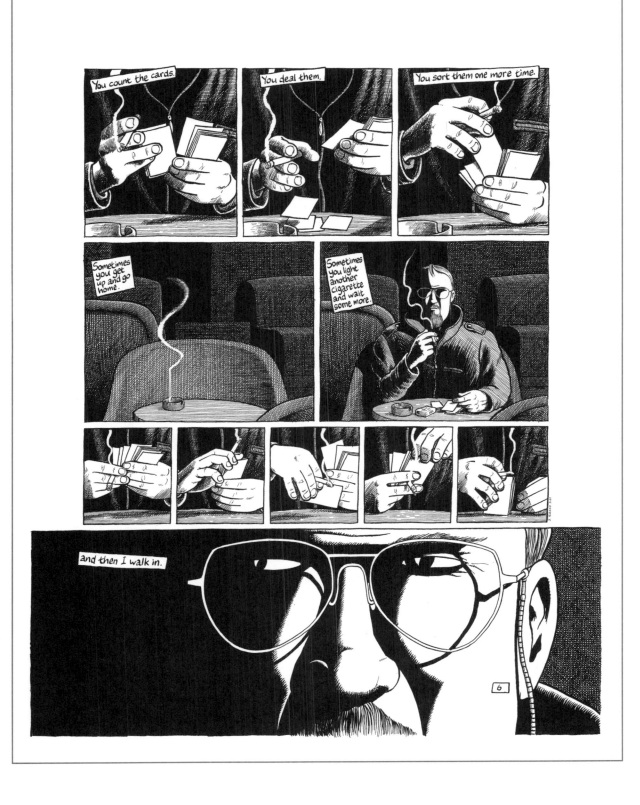

In this later sequence, Neven disdainfully talks of the refugees flooding Sarajevo as life struggles to go on in Bosnia.

Marjane Satrapi

In the second part of her autobiographical account of growing up in Iran and various parts of Europe, Satrapi describes how it was often difficult fitting in with the various social cliques at her school in Austria. The guilt she feels about her newly acquired habits of dressing as a punk and smoking cannabis – while her family remain under the political repression in Iran – is compounded by her denial of her own nationality and rejection of her past. Eventually, the words of her grandmother reassert her self-belief and sense of national identity. Persepolis II: The Story of a Return by Marjane Satrapi, translated by Anjali Singh, copyright © 2004 by Anjali Singh. Used by permission of Pantheon Books, a division of Random House, Inc. Printed with kind permission from Jonathan Cape, London.

from Persepolis II, 2004

I EVEN MANAGED TO DENY MY NATIONALITY.

DURING A PARTY AT SCHOOL.

HI, I'M MARC. I GRADUATED LAST YEAR. YOU'RE NEW! WHAT'S YOUR NAME?

MARJANE. I'VE BEEN HERE A YEAR.

AND WHERE ARE YOU FROM MARIE-JEANNE?

I'M FRENCH.

OH REALLY? YOU HAVE A FUNNY ACCENT FOR A FRENCH GIRL.

OH! I HAVE TO FIND MY FRIENDS. BYE.

I SHOULD SAY THAT AT THE TIME, IRAN WAS THE EPITOME OF EVIL AND TO BE IRANIAN WAS A HEAVY BURDEN TO BEAR.

IT WAS EASIER TO LIE THAN TO ASSUME THAT BURDEN.

WHO'S THAT GUY?

MARC? HE'S ANNA'S BROTHER, THE GIRL IN THE STRIPED SWEAT-ER. HE'S A JERK FROM BOURGE. YOU SHOULDN'T TALK TO THOSE PEOPLE.

AND WHEN I GOT BACK THAT NIGHT, I REMEMBERED THAT LINE MY GRANDMOTHER TOLD ME: "ALWAYS KEEP YOUR DIGNITY AND BE TRUE TO YOURSELF!"

OH GRANDMA ...

David Shrigley

The pieces shown here are taken, in order of appearance, from the following publications: To Make Meringue You Must Beat the Egg Whites Until They Look Like This (Gallery Nicolai Wallner, Copenhagen, 1998); Grip (Pocketbooks, 2000); Centre Parting (Little Cockroach Press, Toronto, 1998) and Blank Page and Other Pages (Modern Institute, Glasgow, 1998). All are untitled.

Untitled, from **To Make Meringue You Must Beat the Egg Whites Until They Look Like This**, 1998

Untitled, from **Centre Parting**, 1998

This ongoing series follows the adventures of the rather dapper Salem Brownstone on his psychedlic descent into a magical world following the death of his father. Nikhil Singh's intensely detailed drawings recall those of Aubrey Beardsley and heighten the decadent nature of the story. "Salem Brownstone is partly a homage to pulp era comics from the 1930s and the horror titles of the '60s," says John Dunning, the writer of the strip. "Having said that, we definitely aim to move beyond these and test the boundaries of the storytelling capabilities of the medium. This is very much a collaboration: I write for Nik's style and his style is influenced by the scripts – a really magical alchemy that never fails to thrill me." In this sequence, the eponymous hero convalesces in a circus trailer before meeting some strange new characters.

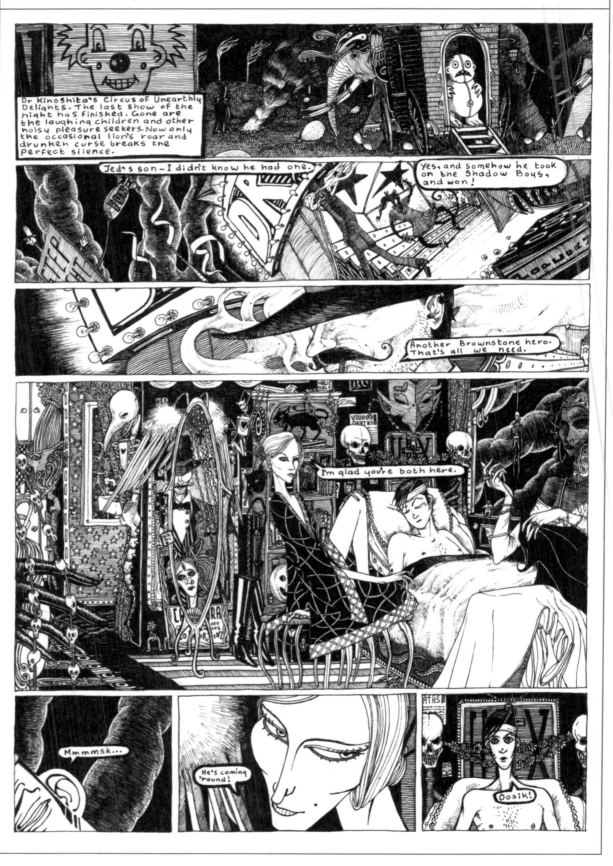

Katja Tukiainen

When Finnish artist and illustrator Katja Tukiainen attended the Lucerne Comic Festival in 2000, she met comic artists Lily Lau (Hong Kong), Markus Hüber (Germany) and Tobi Gaberthuel (Switzerland). The four decided they wanted to create a comic book together. "I suggested the idea of a letter to a dead friend, because I had just lost my dear granny, who was the main character in my comics for many years," explains Tukiainen. "I wrote and drew my 'letter' for my granny, whom I loved and miss so," she continues. "Since then my comics have become more serious and poetic." The resulting work, entitled Letter to a Dead Friend, was published in Lucerne in 2001 by Edition Colomba Urbana. Shown here are spreads from Tukiainen's eight-page contribution entitled For Mumme.

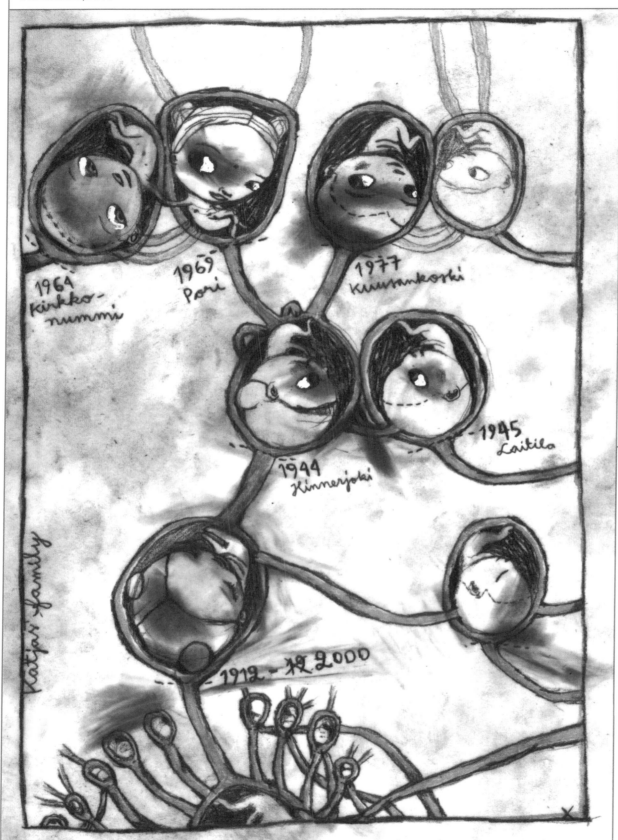

The granny had the heart of a lion. The girl had the

heart of a kitten. Mother and father were at work.

The girl was at work. Then the granny died.

The soft cheeks of the granny were cold and stiff.

The postcard arrived a day too late. The girl was thinking of

the shroud of the granny. The girl sent air mail.

The granny was away.

The girl did not believe it.

Artists' Biographies

 Anna Bhushan UK
Barry Blitt Canada
Fredrik von Blixen Sweden
Mr Clement Hong Kong
Jordan Crane US
Paul Davis UK
Martin tom Dieck Germany
Marcel Dzama Canada
Jeff Fisher Australia
Scott Garrett UK
Tom Gauld UK
Jochen Gerner France
Sammy Harkham US
Igort Italy
Benoît Jacques Belgium
James Jarvis UK
Jason Norway
Andrzej Klimowski Poland
Simone Lia UK
Lorenzo Mattotti Italy
Roderick Mills UK
Ethan Persoff US
David Rees US
Barnaby Richards UK
Jenni Rope Finland
Joe Sacco Malta
Marjane Satrapi Iran
David Shrigley UK
Nikhil Singh South Africa
& John Dunning UK
Katja Tukiainen Finland
Andrew Wightman UK
Jim Woodring US

Anna Bhushan **UK**	Barry Blitt **Canada**	Fredrik von Blixen **Sweden**	Mr Clement **Hong Kong**

Bhushan graduated from London's Royal College of Art in 2004, having previously studied for a BA in Illustration at Brighton. She has an Indian father, and her connection to India has had a large influence on her work: as an avid collector of popular art and ephemera from the region, she says that folk-art traditions have inspired her own drawings and paintings. "Often what I find inspiring about a particular genre of popular or folk art is the unself-consciousness and spontaneous energy which gives rise to quirky and beautifully under-worked images, where the focus is on communicating an idea in the most simple and direct way," she says. "For this reason I often prefer the sketches, ideas and unfinished works of painters to their completed paintings." Bhushan is represented by the illustration agency Heart.
helen@heartagency.com

Canadian-born political cartoonist and illustrator Barry Blitt is today based in New York, where he regularly contributes both cover and editorial illustrations to publications including Entertainment Weekly, the New Yorker, the New York Observer, Newsweek, the Wall Street Journal and Atlantic. This year has also seen the completion of a children's book entitled Once Upon a Time, the End. A frustrated piano player since his childhood in Quebec, Blitt today takes lessons from a jazz teacher and enjoys regular jam sessions with a group of New York-based illustrators. Of his passion for drawing, Blitt tells us, "I bring pen and ink wherever I go, so I can draw if I get an idea or want to isolate myself from people."
barryblitt@optonline.net

Fredrik von Blixen is currently studying for his MA in Graphic Design and Illustration at Konstfack University College of Arts, Crafts and Design in Stockholm, Sweden. Prior to returning to study in his native country, he attended the London College of Printing in London. His freelance work has revolved around illustration and moving-image projects (he has previously created TV idents, with self-composed music, and music promos). Von Blixen's illustration and comic work has a cinematic quality to it and his stories Lost and Found make up the second and third parts respectively of a trilogy. Mysteriously, the first part is yet to be written.
f_blixen@hotmail.com

Working out of his birthplace Hong Kong, France and the UK, Mr Clement is an elusive figure who has been exhibiting since 1999. His first comic work, Go to Hell, May!, appeared in 1998. Since then he has written several works – A Bird on my Head, Window and, most recently, The Gorgeous Habour. Mr Clement also makes toys: Astrolapin, the mysterious long-eared character from The Gorgeous Habour, has been made into a 12-inch action figure.
artist@mrclement.com
www.mrclement.com

Anna Bhushan **UK**	Barry Blitt **Canada**	Fredrik von Blixen **Sweden**	Mr Clement **Hong Kong**

Jordan Crane **US**	Paul Davis **UK**	Martin tom Dieck **Germany**	Marcel Dzama **Canada**

A native of Los Angeles, Jordan Crane currently lives and works out of Somerville, Massachusetts. His exquisite homespun tales often have an undertow of bleakness and deal with the harsh truths of reality: love and loss, life and death. The Last Lonely Saturday, his first book, was published by Highwater Books in 2000 and set the tone for his other highly crafted comic-book work. In addition, he also edits, publishes and draws for the acclaimed Non anthology, now in its fifth issue.
jordan@reddingk.com
www.reddingk.com

Paul Davis was born in Paulton, Somerset in 1962. He graduated from the Exeter College of Art and Design in 1985 with a BA in Fine Art before moving to London. Editorial clients have included Creative Review, Time Out, Graphics International, Dazed & Confused, Self Service, I.D., Arena and the Independent on Sunday; Davis also enjoys design and advertising commissions. With numerous international exhibitions of his personal work already under his belt, he has also had two books published: the first, Blame Everyone Else, by Browns, London; the second, Them and US, by Laurence King Publishing in the UK and Princeton Architectural Press in the US. Both books were published last year.
bigorange@btclick.com

Originally from Oldenburg in Germany, Martin tom Dieck studied illustration at the Fachhochschule für Gestaltung in Hamburg, where he still lives and works. As an illustrator and comic artist he has published work in magazines and under his own imprint, which have largely been printed in German and French. He has received the coveted Max und Moritz Preis – the highest honour for German comic art – twice from the Comic-Salon in Erlangen. From his Der Unschuldige Passagier (The Innocent Passenger) debut in 1993 to La FM, his most recently published story, tom Dieck's work relies on an improvisational, almost unconscious approach to drawing which makes his comics akin to enigmatic, dreamlike journeys.
mtomdieck@t-online.de
www.mtomdieck.net

Dzama has exhibited his paintings and drawings extensively in Canada, the US and Germany, and had a show in late 2004, The Last Winter, at London's Timothy Taylor Gallery. He recently moved to New York from Winnipeg, Canada, where he grew up. He graduated with a degree in Fine Arts from the University of Manitoba in 1997 and is a member of the collective group the Royal Art Lodge. His sketches, ink drawings and hand-tinted watercolours (in which he often uses root beer to get the strange grey-brown colour common to many of his pictures) feature strange distorted creatures that invariably inhabit more familiar and recognizable surroundings. Having gained a cult following with Famous Drawings Present: Marcel Dzama (Smart Arts Press) in 1998 and More Famous Drawings (Plug In Editions) in 1999, Dzama most recently published a collection of his work with McSweeney's Books entitled The Berlin Years. "Because of my geographical isolation, most of the news that I hear comes from the radio," says Dzama of the experience of living in his native Winnipeg, before his move to the US. "I think my work reflects that distance. My characters are small, and pretty much out of touch with the rest of the world. When the news is bloody and fearful, my work reflects it."
dzama@mts.net

Jeff Fisher Australia	**Scott Garrett** UK	**Tom Gauld** UK	**Jochen Gerner** France
Jeff Fisher was born in Melbourne, Australia in 1952. He began drawing and designing professionally in the 1970s, after graduating from Melbourne's Preston Institute of Technology. He worked mostly on advertising jobs for clients including Puma and the Victorian Gas Board until in 1981 he moved to the UK and started designing covers for the New Scientist and the New Worker while drawing for papers including the New York Times and the Sunday Times. He has created over 150 book jackets for Bloomsbury Publishing (perhaps most notably for the books of Louis de Bernières, including the hugely successful Captain Corelli's Mandolin) and illustrated books for both the adult and children's markets, and enjoys graphic design commissions. Fisher, who today lives on the edge of the Fontainebleau forest outside Paris with his family, is perhaps happiest, however, when painting for himself and making furniture. j.fisher@wanadoo.fr	Scott Garrett's rather absurdist outlook on everyday life has meant his personal quirks and fantasies have regularly been played out in the pages of the Independent on Sunday in his Parallel Universe column. He studied at Kingston University in London and now enjoys commissions from clients attracted to his unique and witty approach in both the UK and America. The nonsensical nature of everyday life is the main reference for his illustrations, which have run in Time Out, the Guardian and the Financial Times, among others. He is represented by the illustration agency Heart. heart@dircon.co.uk	Scottish illustrator and comic-book artist Tom Gauld has been based in London since he finished an MA at the Royal College of Art in 2001. Using pencil, micro pen and a Mac, Gauld creates witty, beautifully drawn illustrations for clients including Faber & Faber, Penguin, Orange, the New Yorker, the Guardian and Time Out, for whom he produced a comic strip entitled Move to the City. Much of Gauld's time is dedicated to creating comic books: to date he has published five under the Cabanon Press imprint, which he created with Simone Lia. tomgauld@btconnect.com www.cabanonpress.com	Born in Nancy in the east of France to a French father and German mother, Jochen Gerner graduated from the École Nationale des Beaux-Arts de Nancy. He has since lived in Paris, New York, Berlin and Lille but has recently moved back to his home town. Editorial illustration clients have included Libération, Télérama, Le Monde, Nova, Les Inrockuptibles and the New York Times. Gerner also enjoys graphic design commissions, and has contributed to some 20 books published by, among others, Les Editions du Rouergue, L'Ampoule and L'Association. Perhaps happiest when creating his own publications, which range from short comics and children's books to narrative works of over 100 pages, Gerner is inspired largely, he tells us, by "contemporary art, politics, architecture and literature". jochen.gerner@libertysurf.fr

Sammy Harkham **US**	Igort **Italy**	Benoît Jacques **Belgium**	James Jarvis **UK**

Born and raised in Los Angeles, Harkham spent three years studying animation at the California Institute of the Arts, but dropped out before graduating. He edits and draws for his "somewhat annual" comics anthology Kramers Ergot, which is published under his own imprint, Avodah Books. Now in its fifth incarnation, Kramers Ergot's initial issues included work by himself and his friends. More recently, the scope of contributors has grown to include a huge range of comic-book talent. Harkham is currently working on a solo comic series, Crickets.
sammysumo@mac.com

Igor Tuveri, who uses the Igort moniker for his comic-book work, was born in Cagliari in Italy. Moving to Bologna aged 20, he began to publish comics in the late 1970s and '80s. His first stories were published in Il Pinguino (The Penguin) magazine, which he co-founded. His illustrations also appeared in a range of international magazines, such as Linus, Frigidaire and Vanity. More recently he established what is now one of Europe's best comics publishers, the Coconino Press in Italy. In 2003, Igort's first book to be translated into English, 5 Is the Magic Number, was published by Drawn & Quarterly in the US and, alongside other commendations, received the Book of the Year award at the Frankfurt Book Fair and the Grand Prix at the Romic Comics Festival in Rome.
igort@igort.com
www.igort.com

Having spent many years working as an illustrator in the UK, Jacques is regarded as one of the country's foremost artists. He studied in Brussels at the Royal Academy of Fine Arts and then at the Ecole Nationale Supérieure des Arts Visuels de la Cambre, before working at the London-based design consultancy Pentagram for three years. Travelling to the US and Belgium, he then returned to the UK for the next eight years, but since 1991 has been living and working in France. Exhibiting his drawings, paintings and sculpture throughout Belgium and France, he also publishes collections of his work under his own imprint, Benoît Jacques Books. Jacques's drawings have appeared in a range of newspapers and magazines including the Observer, the New Yorker, the New York Times, Die Zeit, Vogue Germany, Libération and El Pais.
Benoit.Jacques@wanadoo.fr

A freelance illustrator since 1995, when he graduated from London's Royal College of Art, Jarvis has enjoyed success both as an illustrator and vinyl-toy designer. His characters frequently bridge the two media and happily exist in both three dimensions and on the page. Jarvis's initial collaborations with the clothing company Silas in 1998 led him to design his first toy figure, based on his character Martin, and in 2000 he exhibited the work completed under the banner of World of Pain at the Parco Gallery in Tokyo, from which sprung the comic of the same name and, later, several other vinyl figures. His toy company, Amos, has produced several series of his In Crowd figures, each of which has been based on a theme: from zombies to teenage juveniles, his three-and-a-half-inch creations have become immensely collectable. Richard Scarry and Hergé are favourites of Jarvis's, as is psychedelia, the great outdoors and, of course, the novels of Jane Austen.
info@amostoys.com
www.amostoys.com

Jason Norway	Andrzej Klimowski Poland	Simone Lia UK	Lorenzo Mattotti Italy
Originally from Molde in north-west Norway, Jason (John Arne Sæterøy) now resides in Oslo where he has lived since attending the Strykjernet art school and the National College of Art and Design. He published his first graphic novel, Lomma full av regn (Pocket Full of Rain), in 1995 and in 1997 released the first of his comic-book series Mjau Beibi (Meow Baby) through publishers Jippi Forlag. Well known for using animals as the characters in his strips and comic books, Jason also used his familiar cast in his ambitious adaptation in 2003 of Jernvognen (The Iron Wagon), the classic Norwegian crime novel by Stein Riverton. He has received commendations from the Norwegian Comics Association, two Sproing Awards for the best Norwegian comic in 1996 and 2001 and two Ignatz Award nominations for his prolific output, published by Jippi Forlag and Bladkompaniet in Norway and by Fantagraphics in the US. mail@jippicomics.com	Designer and illustrator Andrzej Klimowski was born in the UK of Polish parentage. He trained at Central Saint Martins College of Art and Design, then at the Academy of Fine Art in Warsaw, where he also worked professionally. He is currently head of illustration at the Royal College of Art in London. Since the late 1970s, Klimowski has designed posters and book jackets for Faber & Faber and Penguin, as well as completing commissions in editorial design, TV graphics and animation. He dedicates much of his time to self-initiated projects, including short films, illustrations and books, most recently The Secret, published by Faber & Faber. His work, which had previously been largely collage-based, now uses gouache, ink and linocut. "In recent years I have become aware of the quickening pace of fashion and technology. The media world is expanding at breakneck speed and we are drowning in an excess of information, much of which is slight and of no lasting value. My response to this excessive output is to simplify my working methods." andrzej@klimowski.com aklimowski@yahoo.co.uk www.klimowski.com	Artist and illustrator Simone Lia graduated with a BA in Illustration from the University of Brighton in 1995, then gained an MA in Communication Art and Design from the Royal College of Art in London. She occasionally works in advertising, print and editorial, but dedicates much of her time to her own publications. To date she has created four comic books under the Cabanon Press imprint (www.cabanonpress.com), which she created with Tom Gauld. She has written and illustrated four books, for Gullane, David & Charles, Egmont and Methuen, and has also illustrated several children's books for Mammoth. Lia's tools include pencil, dip-pen, paint and a computer, and she has recently been experimenting with screenprinting. simone@simonelia.com www.simonelia.com	Paris-based artist and illustrator Lorenzo Mattotti was born in Brescia, Italy in 1954. Although he graduated from the Facoltà di Architettura (Faculty of Architecture) in Venice, he soon decided to devote himself to comic art. Using chalk, pastels, pen, pencil and paint, he has completed numerous publications, for both children and adults, working alongside comic writers. Mattotti dedicates much of his time to these publications but also works as a fine artist, painting predominantly in acrylic; he has contributed to advertising campaigns and enjoys illustration commissions for clients including Vanity, the New Yorker, Le Monde and the Süddeutsche Zeitung. mattotti@wanadoo.fr www.mattotti.com

Roderick Mills UK	**Ethan Persoff** US	**David Rees** US	**Barnaby Richards** UK

Mills works out of a studio in Hackney, east London. He has completed numerous projects for magazines, newspapers and publishing clients since graduating from the Royal College of Art in 2001. His book-cover work includes The Autograph Man by Zadie Smith while he has illustrated all three volumes of Peter Bowler's The Superior Person's Book of Words and, more recently, contributed to How to Be Idle by Tom Hodgkinson. A spontaneous artist, Mills creates work with an intuitive feel, a quality that is strengthened by his use of disposable pens and Biros and his experiments with reproduction techniques via the photocopier. Currently working on a personal film project commissioned by the Wellcome Trust, he is represented by the illustration agency, Heart, whose book Beat features some of the agency's best work.
helen@heartagency.com

Living and working in Austin, Texas in the US, Ethan Persoff graduated from the Art Institute of Chicago in 1997. His comic work has been published by Fantagraphics and he is well known for his collaborative project Pogostick – a bleak tale of the life and gradual decline of night-time employee Audrey Grinfield – which he developed with artist Al Columbia. His website, www.ep.tc, features numerous comic-book projects along with several examples of his music and writing. While his silent story Teddy is a surreal, sequenced narration incorporating a picnic and a car crash, his longer work A Dog and his Elephant is an emotionally fraught story of abuse within a violent and claustrophobic relationship. This latter work is available to read in full on his website.
epersoff@yahoo.com
www.ep.tc

Today based in Brooklyn, New York, and with a degree in Philosophy from Oberlin College, David Rees grew up reading comic books and put his first "mini-comics" together in the eighth grade. While he tells us that he has always dabbled in cartooning, he admits he never imagined that it would become a career. It wasn't until after the tragic events of 9/11 that Rees discovered the cartooning voice that he was looking for when he started posting his online clip-art strip Get Your War On as a direct result of becoming agitated by world events. Although he had already self-published his comic books My New Fighting Technique Is Unstoppable and My New Filing Technique Is Unstoppable, it was Get Your War On that really got Rees noticed – he currently produces a regular strip for Rolling Stone magazine. All of Rees's personal strips have been published in book form: his first, Get Your War On, by Soft Skull Press in New York and My New Fighting Technique Is Unstoppable, My New Filing Technique Is Unstoppable and Get Your War On II by Riverhead Books, also in New York.
dr@mnftiu.cc
www.mnftiu.cc

Barnaby Richards lives in Cornwall in the UK. A graduate of Falmouth College of Arts' MA Illustration course, he has worked as a freelance illustrator and has also set up his own imprint, Pending Press, through which he published a short work called I Am Inspiration, "a dark little narrative about the nature of inspiration, and the process of translating a thought into words and pictures". The story features a deer-like character (inspiration) who is eventually hunted down by three pen-wielding figures. "The character at the end isn't necessarily dead," says Richards of the transformation that takes place within the comic, "it's just that he has been reduced from something imaginary into something real." Richards is fascinated by medieval art and architecture and enjoys life's more pastoral pursuits. The Funeral, a short work about loss and discovery, draws on these interests and is available through Atlantic Press, while his latest work, Art & Agatha, is set to be published in 2005.
pendingpress@hotmail.com

Jenni Rope Finland	Joe Sacco Malta	Marjane Satrapi Iran	David Shrigley UK
Born in Lahti, Finland in 1977, Jenni Rope is today based in Helsinki, where she works as an illustrator, designer, artist, animator and comic artist. She graduated from the University of Arts and Design, Helsinki in 2002 with a TaK (BA) in Graphic Design and received a Certificate in Animation Production from the London College of Printing in 2000. Prior to this, in 1997 Rope founded her own publishing house, Napa Books, under whose imprint she has since published her own comics, graphic novels and flip books as well as those of other artists. Rope's comics have also been printed in several magazines including Stereoscomics (France) and Bild&Bubbla (Sweden) as well as in books published by L'Association, France, Lapasteque, Canada and Bedeteca, Lisbon, Portugal, among others. Commercial projects include illustration commissions from advertising agencies and record labels. jennirope@hotmail.com www.napabooks.com	Joe Sacco is one of the world's most itinerant comic-book writers, dividing his time between Europe, the Middle East and the US. He attended the University of Oregon, graduated in journalism in 1981 and completed his first comic book two years later in his native Malta. His most lauded work has tended to draw on his experiences in countries such as Israel, Serbia and Bosnia, and he is often described as a cartoonist/journalist (or part of what has been termed the New Journalism scene) as his graphic novels – in particular Palestine, Safe Area Gorazde and The Fixer – have dealt with the experiences of anarchy, war and political upheaval. Sacco combines eyewitness reportage with the medium of comics storytelling in order to explore some of the most emotionally weighty situations. When his Palestine series was published in book form by Fantagraphics it contained an introduction by the critic Edward Said and invited comparisons with Art Spiegelman's Pulitzer Prize-winning Maus. The Fixer, his most recent graphic novel (published by Drawn and Quarterly in the US and Jonathan Cape in the UK), deals with his experiences of the breakdown of civil order in Sarajevo. queries@aragi.net	Currently based in Paris, Satrapi is originally from Rasht in Iran. Moving to Tehran as a child, she was educated at the Lycée Français but left to go to Austria in 1984, spending time in Vienna, then went to Strasbourg, where she studied illustration. Returning to her native country four years later, she once again encountered the harsh realities of a repressive regime – the reason that she originally left Iran. The second volume of her memoir Persepolis looks at this homecoming after her years in Europe. Her work has appeared in newspapers and magazines and she has also written many children's books. When finally completed, Persepolis will comprise four parts, published by Jonathan Cape in the UK and Pantheon in the US. capeeditorial@randomhouse.co.uk www.randomhouse.com/pantheon/	Born in Macclesfield in the north of England in 1968, David Shrigley graduated from the Glasgow School of Art with a degree in Fine Art in 1991 and has since exhibited widely in Europe and North America. Editorial clients have included Esquire, Frieze and the Guardian, and Shrigley has also produced animated pop promos for artists such as Blur and Bonnie Prince Billy. Numerous books of his drawings have been published (details of which can be found at www.redstonepress.co.uk), and Shrigley has also created work in public spaces which he documents photographically. More recently, he has also turned his hand to making sculptural pieces. Today, Shrigley lives and works in Glasgow and is represented by the Stephen Friedman Gallery, London. davidshrigley@btopenworld.com www.davidshrigley.com

Nikhil Singh **South Africa** & John Dunning **UK**

South Africa-based artist Nikhil Singh collaborates with UK writer John Dunning on Salem Brownstone, an ongoing graphic novel that has been serialized in the pages of UK-based comics anthology Sturgeon White Moss. Singh's first graphic novel, entitled Host, was published this year by Bell-Roberts and he also plans to release two "optical singles" with his band the Wild Eyes: each single will be released alongside a two-page comic. Dunning was born in Zululand, South Africa and has written with fellow African comic artist Jason Masters as well as Singh. He now resides in London where he has curated, with Paul Gravett, the nascent Comica festival at the Institute of Contemporary Arts. He now plans to write comics full time.
koicolloidal@inorbit.com
sleekhack@hotmail.com

Katja Tukiainen **Finland**

Finnish comic artist, illustrator and fine artist Katja Tukiainen was born in 1969 in the town of Pori; today she is based in Helsinki. Tukiainen always wanted to be an artist and fell in love with the medium of comic art or narrative illustration after learning to read with her mother's Carl Barks comic magazines. Having studied painting at the Academy of Fine Arts of Venice, Tukiainen went on to complete an MA in Art and Art Education at the University of Art and Design, Helsinki in 1996. Since then she has enjoyed many international solo and group exhibitions. Tukiainen has written several graphic novels and some 44 comic books since 1991, and also finds time to undertake illustration commissions for magazines, children's book publishers and school textbooks.
katjatukiainen@hotmail.com
www.katjat.net

Andrew Wightman **UK**

Much of Andrew Wightman's work looks at intergalactic travel and the nature of man's existence within uncharted space. Hailing from Fife in Scotland, Wightman has worked as an illustrator for clients such as Penguin and Time Out magazine since graduating from the Royal College of Art in London.
andrew@differentthings.com

Jim Woodring **US**

Seattle-based Jim Woodring is originally from Los Angeles and the surreal and psychedelic directions that his art takes owes much to his childhood experiences there.
His earliest attempts at transforming his innermost thoughts into words and pictures came via work published in a weekly tabloid, Two-Bit Comics, and in the Los Angeles Free Press, as well as his own self-published title, The Little Swimmer. Woodring went on to become a freelance cartoonist and published the first of his "illustrated autojournals" entitled JIM in 1980. After working for an LA-based animation studio, a collection of work from JIM was published as a magazine by Fantagraphics. Since then Woodring has concentrated full time on his fantastical branch of cartooning, gaining a faithful following through his much-loved character Frank, whose adventures were compiled in The Frank Book (also published through Fantagraphics). He has recently decided to pursue the creation of single-panel narratives and much of his work can be seen, and indeed bought, from his well-maintained website.
jim@jimwoodring.com
www.jimwoodring.com

Credits	Acknowledgements	Picture Credits

Credits

Published in North America by
Yale University Press
P.O. Box 209040
New Haven, CT 06520-9040
U.S.A.

First published in 2005 by
Laurence King Publishing Ltd
London

Copyright © text 2005
Roanne Bell and Mark Sinclair

Library of Congress Control
Number: 2005926355

ISBN: 0-300-11146-0

Printed in China

Editors/art directors:
Roanne Bell, Mark Sinclair
Design: Brighten the Corners –
Studio for Design, and Tom Gauld
Cover illustration: Tom Gauld
Back cover: Simone Lia

Acknowledgements

Thanks to Tom and Billy; Jo Lightfoot
and Robert Shore at Laurence King;
Gav, Nathan, Pat and Paula at
Creative Review; John Dunning; Dan
Francis at Jonathan Cape; Sylvia
Farago at Sturgeon White Moss;
Eric Reynolds at Fantagraphics;
Peggy Burns at Drawn & Quarterly;
Tom Devlin at Firewater Books;
Gosh Comics in London; Matt at the
David Zwirner Gallery, New York;
Omar at Coconino Press in
Bologna; Eivor at Bladkompaniet in
Oslo; Nicole Aragni; Helen
Osbourne at Heart; Anjali Singh at
Pantheon; Céline Merrien at
L'Association; and Julian
Rothenstein at Redstone Press.
Special thanks to our families
and to Em and Charlie for all the
encouragement.

Picture Credits

Pages 50–51:
Marcel Dzama: Untitled, 2004.
Ink and watercolour on paper,
35.6 × 27.9 cm. A Prospective
Scene in Winnipeg, 2004. Acrylic
on board, 25.4 × 22.9 × 1.9 cm.
Signed, dated, titled verso. Untitled,
2003. Acrylic, paper on board,
22.9 × 25.4 × 0.6 cm. All courtesy
of David Zwirner, New York.